SMACKED

SMACKED

'What we call the beginning is often the end
And to make an end is to make a beginning.
The end is where we start from.' –
TS Eliot 'Four Quartets'

MELINDA FERGUSON

Oshun

Published by Oshun Books
An imprint of Struik Publishers
(a division of New Holland Publishing (South Africa) (Pty) Ltd)
Cornelis Struik House
80 McKenzie Street
Cape Town 8001

First published in 2005

10 9 8 7 6

Publishing Manager: Michelle Matthews
Managing Editor: Ceridwen Morris
Editor: Gwen Podbrey
Designer: Bruce Henderson
Typesetter: Martin Jones
Cover design: Bruce Henderson
Production Manager: Valerie Kömmer

Set in 10 pt on 16 pt Stone Serif
Reproduction by Hirt & Carter Cape (Pty) Ltd
Printed and bound by Paarl Print, Oosterland Street, Paarl, South Africa

ISBN-13: 9 781770 070486
ISBN-10: 1 77007 048 6

www.imagesofafrica.co.za

IMAGES OF AFRICA
PHOTO LIBRARY

To my darling boys James and Daniel,
who are truly the lights of my life

ACKNOWLEDGEMENTS

Thank you Alex for getting clean and inspiring me to do it too, and for giving such a beautiful life to the boys.

Thank you to my dear friends Martine and Rafiq for all the love and support.

Also thanks to: My family Neil, Jeni and Gill, my mother no longer with us, Ivor, Yvonne and the Yazbek family, Jimmy, Joe, Tako, Dave C, Peta, Darryl, Kaz, Jane, Meg, Dr Michael Niss, Alex H, Michelle M of Oshun, Andrew Phillips and Mads and everyone at *True Love* magazine especially Khanyi , Gwen, Glynis and Busi, and Narcotics Anonymous and all the addicts out there worldwide, trying to get clean and stay clean.

And especially – Thank you Mr Ketching(!) – for all the 'how many words have you written?' nudges, the priceless home improvement ideas, the love and great times spent together. May there be many more.

Smacked is based on my memories. In writing this book and living my life, I have undoubtedly hurt or angered some people – I deeply apologise for any pain I have caused.

Enjoy your lives!

PART 1

WHAT WE CALL THE BEGINNING IS OFTEN THE END

CHAPTER 1

SMACKED

I have a gun in my mouth. I don't know much about guns, but the taste of the metal makes me want to gag. It's 1999, 3 am on a Saturday, Hillbrow, Johannesburg and I've never been more terrified in my life.

There are four people in the one-roomed, dingy flat on Soper Road: a Nigerian dealer, two coloured gangstas and me.

'Open your legs,' a surly, scar-faced specimen called Baby Face instructs me. I'm huddled in a frozen ball, my hands pressing my knees together.

'Please don't rape me.' My voice is small. My lips mercury-cold. I'm a broken bird – no crying, just a crackled whimper. Oh God, this can't be happening to me. The terror, the fear gets the better of me. Hysteria rises.

'Shoot me, don't rape me, shootmedon'trapemeshootme.' The words are a desperate mantra. God's not listening.

The gun thuds into my temple. Pistol-whipped. Metal on skull silences me. Blank out.

'I don't like sex,' he grins. 'I like rape.'

He unzips his trousers. It's all slow motion now.

'Please wear a condom,' I whisper.

Weirdly, he obliges. In this moment that is extended like elastic in time, I am vaguely relieved. Safe sex. No diseases. No Aids, gonorrhoea, STDs.

It's insane. I am about to be raped and I am relieved that latex is going to put some weird distance between this sicko and me.

I enter into a place of white noise. The kind when you're a kid and hold a shell against your ear and you hear the sea rushing in, that's the space I go to. I turn my head and concentrate on the floral pattern on the yellowing wallpaper. I know I am defeated. Now I close my eyes. Blank out.

He pulls my stockings down and he rapes me.

It's strangely silent, unemotional. There is no violence, no struggle. Just empty blank. He is weak; cocaine cock can't do much, pushes pathetically into me. Sad stocking sausage. It doesn't last long. Maybe three minutes.

I turn to the side and see the other two watching. I know they are coming to get me.

'Condoms,' I say. 'Please wear.'

They oblige; one by one they move to me. It's like a weird, ominous dance, slow motion. I am on an altar, a sacrifice, and they are penetrating me in some kind of symbolic hatred against all women. Maybe they just want to get laid. Who knows?

Are they having a good time, I wonder? What are they getting out of this? Do they like me? Do they think I'm fat?

This must be the most unsexual, unerotic experience. It's like fucking a dead person – necrophilia. Maybe they like that.

All these things go round and round in my head while one by one they rape me.

The whole experience is over in less than 30 minutes. That's all the time it's taken to change me forever. Now I am raped. It hits me dull force. I am a zombie, dead. I am cut off, truncated to the core.

It's over. I go into the bathroom. I run a hot bath. I need something to burn me, clean it all away. The condoms are left lying near the bed. Pathetic drooped latex near the cigarette butt-burnt plastic dustbin.

My head is showing swelling, bruising. The eyes that stare back at me in the murky bathroom mirror are not mine. The steam is washing everything I knew about me away. I know I am never, ever, ever going to be the same again.

I lie in the water. I get out. I put on my clothes, pull on my stockings. I go back to the bedroom. They are smoking. My rapists give me a rock. Crack cocaine, my reward. I smoke it greedily on the glass pipe. Some call it sucking the devil's cock. It is, it is.

It is this little white drug that has brought me to this place, this hell.

Three weeks ago I was a mother, a housewife, a poet living in a four-bedroomed house in the North West. I had a full-time maid, a husband, a washing machine, two sons, a drug habit and a percolator.

Now I am raped. It feels like a career description: 'What are you?' – a question to be asked at cocktail parties, glasses tinkling. Pause. 'I am raped.'

Now my addiction to crack keeps me in this room with my rapists. I share more drugs. Soon it's as though nothing has happened. They seem nonplussed by the events of half an hour ago. They laugh and speak, referring to me intermittently. I seem to be forgetting quickly too! If I block it all out and take loads of drugs right now, perhaps it will be like this has never happened. Perhaps I will forget it all.

As I bend down to suck the pipe and feel my heart race triple speed, I think … 'What you really need now is a hit of heroin, some smack.'

'Can you organise some brown for me – you know, heroin? I need to come down,' I whisper to no-one in particular.

_____

My relationship with heroin began in 1993, as a flirtation.

'This is the baddest, worstest, most pushing of the limits of life,' I think secretively, hugging my tummy that has for the last hour been heaving merrily into a rust-orange, urine-stained toilet bowl.

All from smoking a single line of brown liquid, gliding like a snake dragon slowly … Tinfoil catching the glint of a single candle, blowing weakly in the large, dank lounge of a draughty, pre-election unrenovated house in Yeoville.

'This stuff is amaaazing!' I sigh languidly. Sarah Bernhardt to herself. Mata Hari in an opium den. Maud Allan. It's just me and the brown and Lou and the darkness of the Velvet Underground.

I've never met a junkie who liked light. You can't. It reminds you too much of the other world, the 'real world', the world of tomorrow, later, sometime, soon, whenever … 8–4 jobs, insurance, medical aid, 2.5 kids, Aids, policies for life, death, hail, rain, cancer, kids, education, plastic surgery, space insurance if you hurt your foot on Jupiter or Mars. So much fucking insurance it made me hurl, bring up again.

———————————

I had recently travelled to Europe with my boyfriend, Boy 2. We had won first place in a local film competition and, as part of the prize, we were awarded a free passage to Europe to attend a prestigious film festival in Germany. From being a little sheltered white chick in SA, now – like a cooing pioneer – I suddenly found myself raving on foreign soil: all my hunger and thirst for knowledge of 'out there', away from the laager of our oppression, made me want to eat and gulp and chew and swallow everything that was possibly on offer.

I dropped my first E in London in a club called Heaven and experienced pure Ecstasy! Coming home, two months later, I wanted to spread that vibe, be at the forefront of cool and embrace all that our country's imminent freedom was about to symbolise.

So when I came across the heroin, 'smack', 'brown' or 'horse', as some call it, there was nothing to do but jump on its back, dig my heels in and spur it on full speed ahead into a delicious yi-haa canter!

———————————

We're at Matt and Winn's house. They're the couple who've been kind enough to invite us into their sordid little ring of poppies, their little seedy lives. Like bone-hungry vampires, they get to Boy 2 first. About six weeks back, I think; times and dates seem hazy now.

Boy 2 and I had been seeing each other for just on a year and we were in love and inseparable. We had always done everything together, slept, woken, eaten, worked, travelled, laughed, played pool – we were one of those perfect couples who loved each other's company, an almost Siamese connection: joined at the hip, I suppose.

Then one night, he didn't come home. I sat up waiting. The clock said 2.30 am. We did not own cellphones back in '93, so I couldn't call. I naturally assumed something dreadful had happened to him. I phoned all the hospitals I could think of and then finally, not driving myself, I decided to take a walk around Yeoville to see if I could find him.

When I walked past a house in St George's Street and I saw his small orange Datsun, my heart all but leapt out my chest. Thank God! I had found him. I ran down the driveway to the back of the house, where I saw a light burning. It was 3 am and most of the neighbouring houses were in darkness.

Something made me slow down as I approached what seemed to be the kitchen window. I looked through. Boy 2 and a good-looking, dark-haired man were hunched over something. I inched closer, staring through the window, my breath misting the pain.

They were holding a square of tinfoil and Boy 2 had a silver tube in his mouth. The 'looker' was holding a lighter and he was steering the flame from beneath, which seemed to be burning something, on the foil. Smoke was rising and Boy 2 was inhaling.

I stood transfixed by the sight. I saw Boy 2 close his eyes, inhale and really slowly exhale – and when his eyes opened, I will never forget the look I saw in them. It was the most peaceful and happy I had ever seen him. It was a look that said: 'I have everything. I am complete. I am in heaven.' It was a look that said: 'I don't need you.'

I didn't know that they were smoking heroin, chasing the dragon, but I do know something chilled me right to the inside of my bones. I knew right then I should turn around, walk back down the driveway, back down the road to the flat we shared, up the stairs to the cupboard, pack my belongings and get the fuck out of there.

I knew in that moment I was at a crossroads and if I entered that space, my life was about to change direction completely. It terrified me – the hugeness of the absolute knowing. I'm four again, the ceiling's towering higher, me getting smaller. Little Alice caught in terror zone. Heart beating, drum drum drum. It's frozen out here on this sweaty summer night.

And then, as though I had no choice, propelled by something deeper, I walked forward, tapped on the window, my breath made foggy clouds on the glass. I said: 'Can I come in? Please.'

Six weeks later we are visiting them nearly every day of the week.

————————————

Matt and Winn have fuck-all money.

'Skint,' Matt grins. He's been in London for three years, that's where he's picked up the habit. His homecoming brings happy, shining people having fun. Happy heroin for some.

They're skinny but weirdly beautiful, like two greedy rattlesnakes, hungry for a hit. Matt is just plain absolutely fucking gorgeous. He's like the Angel of Death, just more beautiful. Irish-Lebanese eyes. Laughing.

He is beautifully terrible. He pulls and pushes, teases and squeezes. He takes and takes and takes and then spits it all out.

Beautiful poison.

Mr Memememememe. Baby man in big body. Needy little Eraserhead yelping like a demented preacher inside. And all Matt's baby beast dragon wanted was smackcracksmack cracksmackcrack. He could manipulate just about anyone into being his proud, privileged provider. He was the world's best pimp. Of himself.

He never had any of his own money and Boy 2, who was a real sucker sometimes, just had to go and get sucked. And I followed like a goose to water. No, rather a sheep to the slaughter.

Matt is a huge, puffing fire horse. But he's also a crab, Cancer.

Beware of crabs. Scavenger survivors. As soon as the ship goes down, they retire to their shells. Oblivious, conscienceless.

A symbiotic relationship develops between the four of us, mostly to Matt and Winn's advantage.

If I say: 'No, Matthew. I will not lend or give you any money,' he'll come in really close, stroking me with those eyes, flirting and say: 'Don't be so tight, luv.' Big grin. *When Irish Eyes are Smiling* echoes round and round.

Being half-Scottish (third generation), he pushes all my 'scared-to-be-stingy' buttons. It's hard to refuse such a shiny horse.

———————

They drive past hotels, motels, Holiday Inn. *'Say if your girl starts acting up, then you take her friend'* is blaring on the car radio as Boy 2's hands nervously clutch the sweaty steering wheel of his old Datsun. His specs are steamed up in dread. Woody Allen in Hillbrow.

He has become Matt's taxi-hearse. Driving him to dark destinations: the Mountbatten, the Sands, The Statesman and other seedy, inner-city, neon-lit destinations. Hotel. Motel. Holiday Inn.

Each time Matt would swagger, guiding pointy London leather boots up to the 13th floor. There with his new friends, the Nigerian drug dealers, he would sample their goods as though he was some kind of fucking winklepicking smack salesman.

Like a vacuum-cleaner he would snort the joint up. And all the time he'd be acting like the dealers should be privileged or something just to have him in the vicinity. An hour or so later, he'd saunter down to Boy 2, who'd be almost crouching on the floor of the little car, ghetto terrified. Bleeding knuckles. Gnawing anguish.

Nicely pinned, Matt would direct Boy 2 home. Then suddenly it was as if he was on some cross-border mission raid – waves of paranoia coming in as fast as uninvited tsunamis, convinced that every vehicle was a cop car, every pedestrian a narc, he'd get more and more manic.

Speedballing silly, he'd roll onto the pavement, mock leopard-crawl into the lounge, turn all the lights off, close the curtains. The enemy was at hand.

And there we'd wait expectantly for the drugs to begin, while Matt played out his paranoid delusions. I thought this to be all rather hilarious – how could anyone be that crazy?

Finally, after much fuss of preparing the paraphernalia (candles, flex, glass tubes, tinfoil, lighters) for our ritualistic rendezvous with death, we humble subjects would be afforded a single chase of heroin melted on foil, or a tiny snippet of crack cocaine smoked through a glass pipe, while he greedily hogged the rest, funded by us, with Winnie in their dank bedroom.

From that one small hit of smack I'd feel woozy, anaesthetised and oblivious to anything outside. A deep,

deep peace would cover me, melt into every cell of my body. Involuntarily my eyes would close and I would make love to Serenity in the heady clouds of Nirvana. Time would be of no consequence: hours and years could drip by like some sweet, surrealist Dali and nothing – no, nothing – in the world out there could come in.

And then, like some hidden cobra lying in sullen wait, my stomach would contract and the puking would begin. On hands and knees, my arms embracing my new lover, the rust-orange stained bowl, the rising of the bile of nothingness, snake heaving out of my being, like a toxic tantrum yelping to get out. That post heroin-hit vomit, it got me every time … my body just didn't seem to want it, but in my 'never-say-no' manner, like all good soldiers of smack, persist I did.

CHAPTER 2

HANGING ON

Winn just hung on.

'I'm not an addict.' She'd wheeze, cockney cough out of her smoky lungs, screwed and tight red in the face. Lying in bed all day, waiting for Matt to return with gear in hand. Passing the time, glancing at the gate. The clock. Clutching the *YOU* magazine in her hands like it's some kind of bible. Watching those soapies, *The Bold*, *The Days*, *The Restless* and all the re-runs.

Until Matt would finally appear. Swashbuckling pirate. Home from great adventures, in the sea of taxis, sidewalks, Berea, Hillbrow – concrete ghetto – Little Lagos. New Pick 'n Pay of drugs. Any-ting you want, Berea, Hillbrow have, like some generous, callous motherfucker.

Mostly sold by Nigerian intelligentsia, Abacha's exiles – teachers, engineers, doctors, lawyers, nice normal people, trying to find a place in the sun ... Finding instead the concrete cul-de-sac of 'Brow Town where to sell the toxic shit to fill the lungs, the veins, to fill the belly, seems like the only plan when cash is *de rigeur*.

The contradiction: going to mosque or church once a week, prayers every day. Looking east, on knees five times a day. Sending wads of American dollars to their beleaguered wives up north, every month, and dealing in death every day. In the real world. In search of their pot of gold. In one of Africa's richest cities: Jo'burg, Jabuva, Jabulani, Motherfuckerstadt.

Found on the sweaty bones of gold and blood and cards and booze and drink and drugs and women and money – loads and loads and loads of glittering nuggets. Glinting gold. Thieves, chancers, swindlers, millionaires made overnight.

And in the new millennium, a century later, it's the same old story – except the rocks being sold are not nuggets, but pathetic little pieces of crack cocaine or little plastic squishy heaps of dust, opium dust. We don't dig for gold – we shove it all up our noses, down our lungs, into our veins. The most addictive drugs of our modern age – our city's getting rich on – and we're getting fucked by.

———————

It was April '94. Jo'burg. Pre-election time. South Africa's first free democratic election ever! In 1994! FUCKKK!!!! WOWE-E-E!!!!

And we sure as hell needed something to take the stress away: after the pain of the long wait, the longest, driest white season of injustice was finally at an end. The fascist rule was over!

'Fuck, we are *so* behind the rest of the world,' I said as I joined the global network. By chasing the dragon I was reaching out to Pakistan, India, Japan, Chile, Columbia, LA, London, Budapest, Moscow, New York. I was part of the commonwealth of culture 'From Yeoville to China' – shoo-wow, great movie.

'The line between being a girl addict and a whore is very fine …' I think as we drive slowly past street whores in crocheted nippy little tops. Now we're scoring five or six times a day.

Soper Road specials. Smackheads. Crackheads. Black heads, white heads, pink heads, blue heads. Pinko's, smacko's, cracko's, jacko's. Any-ting goes.

'Of course! Smack!' I think. 'It's the only way they can bear to shove those blue cheesy dicks, caked with last whore's cum, into their poor stretch-infested mouths. Or in their cunts or whatever other orifice the customer and his kingly prick desires to drip drip drop. For R50 or R30 or maybe even R10. A hit for a fuck, blow, mind out, whatever.

Heroin is weird. It gives you so much pain. But it's the only thing that can take that pain away.

I think of shiny, happy people having fun. *Meet me in the park, people –*' I hum to myself with REM. It's a sunny, beautiful, happy, hilarious day. It's 26 April 1994, the day before the great election, and it's time to celebrate!

'If your name's Ray, then my name's Roy,' said Boy 2 when he met Nigerian Ray. All the Nigerians pick names when they come here and become dealers: Paul, Chris, Ray, Dave … and so on. We know there is no way their Ibo mothers said: 'Oh, today I am going to call my little baby "Ray"' – but, hey, whatever.

Boy 2 is waiting in the car, looking like a nervous wolf into his side mirror, grey hair glinting in the sun on his young, beautiful face, big, sad eyes stare ahead, into nothingness.

I'm skipping off to meet Ray like I'm Dorothy on the yellow brick road. We connect, two souls in space. 'So how can you sell drugs and be such a devout Muslim at the same time? Hey, Ray? How can you ... hey?'

He glares at me, pulls at his fez. He doesn't like this whole scene, he doesn't like the questions, the police coming in, bastard dogs, breaking the door down, terror tactics. Bashing his flat in, his face in, only leaving once their palms are dripping in silver. Lots of it. Taking, taking, fucking him and his brother Karrim up. Allah, where are You? Someone, some addict was setting him up, the crack was starting to get to him. Maybe it was her, Roy's bitch.

'So how does that work, hey?' I shout across valleys and plains, so the whole street can hear, freaking him out, teasing him. 'I mean, you being so religious and all, praying to Allah three times a day, with your shaven head turned towards the east ... On Fridays all morning in mosque. Do you know how long I have to wait for you on a Friday?' Now I'm really on a roll!

Ray spits out the drugs, snugly safe in little pieces of Checkers plastic. He leaves mid-sentence. Looking back quickly over his shoulder. His own demon monkey chasing him.

I grab the drugs, recoil at the feel of slimy saliva all over my hand. I feel the bumps in the mother plastic. Three rocks, three brown.

Perfect symmetry. Yipppe-e-ee, it's party time. Ray answers his phone on the other side of the street and straightens his fez.

I'm not addicted – I keep it a top national secret. Denial sets in and I water her daily, tend to her with devotion, but deep inside I can't lie anymore, 'cept in bed like Winn, nose running, doing the *YOU* blockbuster, modern-day psalms clutched desperately in fearful, empty hands.

And so all that started in glowing, painless Icarus heavenly blissful free fall gliding, whelping to the heavens on trips of true omnipotent soaring, in an instant turned into cold curdly mud sludge porridge, infested by swelling black maggots, swirling and chewing glugs, eating away like cancer black holes on some primordial wasteland. Growing dependency led to growing indecency and addiction moved in to stay.

First thing in the morning needing a hit so bad, body screaming from the sweat sick torture rack of withdrawal and craving, you'll do just about anything to get it. Lies were easy. 'We've got this *bi-i-ig-g* cheque coming,' we say to the ever-impatient Nigerian, who loves money as much as we love brown and white.

We shared a single-minded devotion between dealer and junkie – one of the most reliably persistent relationships known to mankind. And we blamed him for all our troubles, which began to increase with regularity. That's the thing with junkies: it's always something or someone else's fault ...

Druggies stick to each other like rancid fly shit and blame everybody else. They lie around, wingeing and snivelling and moaning, human frailty personified, hypochondriac hypodermic hellsloths. 'It's everybody else's fault!' is our favourite mantra.

So who *is* to blame, then? Mother? Father? Nigerians? Matt? Kurt Cobain? The system? Blame it on circumstance? Blame it on consequence? Better yet, blame it on sheep.

A CURSORY LOOK AT SHEEP

For me, becoming a drug addict was to escape the flocky flock flock. I wanted to be different, stand out from the crowd, be somebody, be counted. Oh, yes, what a noble aim ... but in the end I turned into a shadow, a sheep in rebel's clothing, but a sheep nonetheless.

And once on the outside, I began to crave that flock, to fit in, have a family, a community, a feeling of togetherness, something that would fill that big hole that grew and grew with every hit I took.

Instead I landed up alone at the table with heroin, skipping the starters, main course, dining only on the dessert of brown, eating, breathing, living, dying, shitting heroin.

Boy 2 sat at the other end of that table and our chairs grew further and further apart, more estranged, and all that love we once had flew flighty free out the window, never ever to return.

We became the sheep of silence, catatonia carcasses, blind statues. Boy 2 built fortresses of stony nothingness. I pushed tweaked pinched, hoping to get a reaction. Anything. I was a gnawing gnat brat. I scrawled my thoughts on scraps of paper searching for sanity.

My mouth shut like a clam. Like a nail in the palm, the silence
aches its stringencies. Pull pushes at my paper thick ribs.
Nib, nib, nibble over a quibble a squibble a word a thought
a fear.
Twang! The violin horse hair breaks echoes in the air.

Oh dear someone spilt the milk all over the orange tiles.
It spreads its sourness in the cracks, it smacks of aridness. My
mouth feels dry, I cry and cry. Why do we stay and blink at the
bad painting above the bed?

Maybe it's just my head I think.
You watch cricket cricket cricket
The West Indies win, we can't spin.

I think I'm going mad frill from this bad line
That crackles obscurity between your chair and mine.

———————

It's 10 May 1994, the Inauguration Day of our new president, Nelson Mandela. We are snivelling in a heap of withdrawal. We don't have money for a hit. We are watching the television as planes fly overhead in the cobalt-blue sky, and our new flag flies, fluttering in the wind. The hero of the day stands up and with quiet dignity he speaks to our nation. Our noses run, bodies ache. We lie in a sweatball heap of withdrawal, while the nation swings and jives.

The president talks, his grey hair glimmers in the sun like a halo. 'We ask ourselves: "Who am I to be brilliant, gorgeous, talented fabulous?" Actually, who are we *not* to be? You are a child of God. Your playing small does not serve the world. There is nothing enlightening about shrinking so that other people won't feel unsure around you. We were born to make manifest the glory of God that is within us. It is not in some of us – it is in everyone.'

Fuck! I can't stand it any longer, I feel my muscles tearing up, ripping to pieces from within. I pull the plug on the television. Nelson is snuffed out.

'Come, let's take this to Karrim and swop it for some smack. We can get it back tomorrow, but now I *really* need a hit.'

CHAPTER 3

DADDY

Sometimes in life you latch onto something – you may not be sure why, really, but it worms itself into your being: it may be a line of a song, a poem, a painting or a piece of music. Mine was *Daddy*, by Sylvia Path. The moment I read that poem, I could not keep it out of me – the resounding rhythm that will invariably invade my brain is:

You do not do,
you do not do anymore black shoe,
in which I have lived like a foot
for thirty years,
poor and white,
barely daring to breathe or achoo.

It has followed me everywhere.

'My father died when I was four' is another one of those lines to haunt me through much of my life …I don't remember much about my dad, more like a hazy photo, a little film clip of an event: The Day He Died.

Yet this one day has been a trigger for much of what I term my sick or toxic behaviour over the last 30-odd years.

A junkie will usually find a whole lot of factors on which to blame their addictive behaviour. I have often blamed my drug-using, my inability to sustain healthy relationships with men, with my mother, teachers, my children on this pivotal event ... Who knows whether any of that is really true? What I do know is that the death of him was an event that changed everything ...

It was a typical Saturday afternoon in '70s sunshine, Chevrolet, *braaivleis* South Africa. I sat with him under a newly-planted peach tree. It was me, him and my dolls. It felt perfect. We were having a picnic in the pink plastic tea set I'd got for Christmas. It wasn't real tea, just play-play – sand and water. It tasted yucko, but my dad was sweet and he pretended really well. His large frame sweated and shuddered and shook like a big mudslide with each shovel of sand he dug ... the home for the blossoming tree had to be deep so the roots could really dig in, he told me.

There was a rugby match on the radio in the dining room, to which he would go inside to listen, every now and again. The Springboks *vs* the Lions.

'Everyone hates the English,' my mother had said earlier. I don't believe everything she says, she always talks like she knows it all and sometimes I feel like saying: 'No, it's not necessarily so – surely there are more people out there in the world than just here in South Africa. How do you know *everyone* hates the English?'

But I keep quiet and think these thoughts to myself, because I'm actually quite scared of her, she's German and sometimes she looks like one of those SS guards outside the gas ovens where they sent the Jews to in Auschwitz. I know this because lately I have been looking at the books in the lounge ... they are called encyclopaedias and although I can't really read, my older sister read the words next to the picture when I asked her to, two weeks ago.

I like learning new things, especially on our radio, which is very important in our home. We love to gather round it at night, sit together and listen to *The Mind of Tracey Dark, Check Your Mate ... Squad Cars ...* On Friday nights my dad buys us each a chocolate and we sit around that radio as though we're sitting in a church, quiet and reverent.

My dad worked in a bank and my mom – after dropping out of Wits University – had begun working in the same bank, and that's where she met my dad.

The earliest memory I have of myself is the day I was born. I have been hung upside down by the nurses, to clear the phlegm from my throat. I am a few hours old ... I turn red, then purple – I begin suffocating. My mother wakes to see me struggling for breath – she rings for the nurses. In the nick of time I am rescued and brought back to life ... I often wonder if I confuse the two from this point on and seek death instead of life as hard as I can for the next 33 years.

Now I'm back at the tree ... notice my dad's been gone a long time. Where is he? I pad with my chubby little four-year-old legs towards the kitchen ... A strange panic grips me, tightens around my chest ... My legs begin to move faster and faster. I'm running now, racing up the stairs, leading to the kitchen, gasping, breathing, running ... I all but trip, stumble through the kitchen door ... I see his hulking back in the dining room. He bends towards the radio ... Oh, thank God – my dada's okay! In slow motion, he reaches for the knob, and then BANG CRASH HELL he falls like a giant ... like Plath's big Frisco seal. Down! He's out for the count ...

The Springboks score a winning try! The crowd crackles wild on that old radio ... It seems they are cheering my father's fall ... On the way down, his hand has pushed the knob full volume. Static screams into this Saturday afternoon. He does not move – I move forward. I look slowly at his face. His glass eye stares unmoving. (His real one – scraped out in a rugby scrum back in '55.) Now this one glares ahead.

In the other room my mother's shrill laughter on the phone to a family friend ...

The noise of my dada crashing shakes her out of hyaena-dom. In she runs ... I stand back, silent. Her screaming face contorts towards me. Oh my God, what have I done? The blood is racing through my head, my horse hoof heart, beating, like it does on an amyl trip ... Then the outside chaos, the noise erupts. Panic pancakes through the air; the phone begins to ring.

My little brother and I are hustled off to the neighbours. Ambulance sirens rip the late afternoon canvas of silence. Shepherded like sheep to the slaughter, we watch from the living room window though half-drawn netted curtains ... We race dinky cars down the long corridor passage-way, up and down, down and up. The screech of wheels squeal the hours away. In the dank, gloomy evening I am mesmerised by the glass-like nothingness of it all ...

My dad is taken away. He's gone now. Never to be seen again. And no-one tells us a thing. The wail of the receding ambulance gets dimmer and dimmer ...

And all I can think of in my four-year-old world is: why didn't I do something, why didn't I stop this? It's all 'cos of me my dad is dead, 'cos I was too late ...

This feeling of misplaced guilt will follow me like a sick shadow for the next 30-odd years.

So all that was good turns sour in a matter of hours and I know my world is never, ever, ever going to be the same again. The cobwebs of gloom set into our household ... in one sad day we have become the *Railway Children*, Alcott's *Little Women* – victims of this huge, unnatural disaster ...

My mother is 33; she's burdened with four children under the age of 10. She starts drinking. It starts after the funeral. She hits the bottle for the next 38 years at 4 pm, sometimes earlier, like clockwork every day. She doesn't stop.

Everything changes in our home after my father dies. I become listless and slide down walls and look at high ceilings that stretch higher and higher into the sky of Babel. I call it the Alice Syndrome – where Alice gets smaller and everything around gets bigger and bigger. Like some little crippled bunny, I know I cannot leave this hole, this borough of sadness called *Home Sweet Home* – it says so on a sign next to the flying ducks above the mantlepiece.

There is terrible resignation for a child whose eyes have been opened too early and where there is a deep and dark realisation that there's absolutely no escape, nowhere to go.

Sometimes I find her passed out in the bath at 8 pm, the half-finished glass of wine still cocked in her hand, casting a shadow on her naked stomach, skin distended by five pregnancies. I am always simultaneously terrified and revolted by the sight of my mother, who in real life is capable and efficient, like this – undignified and dead to the world. I always try to wake her up, afraid she may slide under the water, dissolve down the drain and drown, like some slippery seal. She mutters and babbles like she's lost in a deep fog, when she comes to her senses. I never can sleep until I hear her pull the plug and hear the bathroom door open.

She has lost her husband, her father and her tiny daughter Marianne all in the space of three years... her baby Marianne, born in '65 – a year before me – with a hole in her heart, two years before Dr Chris Barnard performed his historic first heart transplant.

Marianne was born two years too early. There was no miracle op for her. She slowly turned blue and my mother watched her precious angel eke out raspy butterfly breaths until, like a sad popped plastic bag, the little one suffocated to death.

Perhaps all this dying made my mother's heart break, never to be mended. It was only the burn of alcohol that could comfort, dull and pickle her feelings right out of her, and take her to the painless place of Elastoplast Wine Land.

There are days when I find glasses of alcohol stashed behind books and photographs of baby Marianne. My heart always dips when I see them, because I sometimes pretend my mother doesn't drink; that she's normal, like my friends' mothers and mothers on TV and in the movies. That's why I hardly ever ask my friends to sleep over, because they will see what she is really like – a slurry, cut off and nonsensical drunk.

We grow more and more isolated. On the outside everything looks fine: we are neatly dressed, brushed and cleaned and sent off to school every day, like shiny, polished shoes.

I achieve. I excel. I bring my mother home reports that are littered with As. I get medals and certificates – I bring them home like a wise man's gift of myrrh to my mother, hoping and praying if I am awarded enough, if enough accolades pile up, I will make my mother so proud and happy that she will never have to drink again. I try and try and try and she drinks and drinks and drinks. And like beans in soil, my anger and helplessness grow and grow, watered only by her sour wine.

The child who has been brought up in the alcoholic family begins to develop a paticular disorder and seems to universally display characteristics carved out from witnessing the alcoholic parent's unmanageability.

Adult Children of Alcoholics (ACOA), like Alcoholics Anonymous, is yet another 12-step group specifically formed to support those who suffered through parental alcohoism. Some of the characteristics found in ACOA are:

1) We became approval-seekers and lost our identity in the process.
2) We are frightened by angry people and any personal criticism.
3) We get guilt feelings when we stand up for ourselves instead of giving in to others.
4) We become addicted to excitement.
5) We have stuffed our feelings from our traumatic childhoods and have lost the ability to feel or express our feelings because it hurts so much.
6) We judge ourselves harshly.
7) We have low self-esteem.

And so the list goes on.

In our woundology-driven world, it is easy to over-identify with every syndrome there is out there, but somehow, each one of the ACOA characteristics speaks particularly strongly to me. Especially the one that says: *'We are dependent personalities who are terrified of abandonment and will do anything to hold onto a relationship in order not to experience painful abandonment feelings which we received from living with sick people who were never there for us emotionally.'*

My mother's drinking changed everything and began to mould into the very heart and mind of me.

And so, despite all evidence of what alcohol does to my mother, at the age of 10, I take my first drink, steal it from the wooden sideboard liquor cabinet where my mother keeps the booze … Addiction is not a rational disease. It's in my bones, you see, the alcohol gene - the one that has outstretched little embracing feelers for that warm liquid that nulls and dulls and makes me feel like everything is going to be okay.

After that first mouthful, it feels like – oh, God, why have I waited for so long? It's a spiritual experience, a slow dance in Eden. It's sweet and warm, lovely – like the long-awaited mother's milk I have been deprived of. I have another, then another ... I can't get enough of the stuff. I am home, dry and soon very drunk ...

By the time I'm in high school, I'm a full-blown teenage alcoholic.

TEENAGE ALCOHOLICS

My best friend Gail and I hide bottles of red wine in garden shrubs at school and drink like little fish at break time. After school we go to Gail's house and close her bedroom door and giggle and drink and carve the names of boys we love on our arms with compasses. It feels like everything's possible when we are sweetly intoxicated. The world is at our feet. Gail's mother comes in one day and accuses us of being 'lesbians' – she says the word with an ugly snarl on her lip. I'm not even sure what she means – but it sounds like something horrible. No matter. We giggle when she goes out and take another swig. We make blood sister pacts to never, ever leave each other ...

We start clubbing, late nights leapt out of bedroom windows, pale-faced Goths, wanna-be punks, our make-up thick, our lips dark maroon, we are free – virgins on the highway to heavenly hell. We're 14, punk is big – Sid Vicious says: 'Nevermind the bollocks'; Kurt will later have the same sentiments, with the hugely popular *Nevermind*. And from the deep southernmost point on the African continent, cut off from civilisation, I cast my eyes north and look to everything from the island of England to be hip, cool and aspirational. Sid kills himself, what a drag! But then, of course, there's always Bob.

CHAPTER 4

BOB MARLEY'S DEAD!

On 11 May 1981, we are devastated to hear before school on the local radio station that the king of reggae, Bob Marley, is dead. *No woman no cry* Bob, *I wanna love you and treat you right* Bob. Oh my God! What happened to **BOB!!?**

At break Gail and I congregate at the cricket pavilion, cut chunks of our hair, add a dash of red wine, stolen from her father's cabinet, put it all on a heap of twigs. On top we place a picture of Bob and then light the whole damn sacrifice and watch those orange flames lick and devour it all. Our hero is dead. We wail for our Marley.

We smash a black vinyl of Bob's *Exodus* and swig on the hip flask of wine. We seem to be the only ones who are devastated by the news. But, then, we're different to the rest of them – we like Linton, Peter, Jimi, Marvin and Bob ...

'Kaffir-lover!' the boys sometimes snigger as I walk into school. 'Have you kissed your garden boy today?' they taunt.

I ignore them, pity them, because they're the ones who are potato-head, racist blockheads ... if they only knew that the world was much bigger than South Africa, then maybe they'd see the light. I refer to the whole lot of them as the interbred, sad, poor trailer park trash.

I feel superior in my enlightenment. I never doubt that I am right. Which is weird, I suppose, because the walls in my home are papered with racist under- and overtones. My mother – a Nazi sympathiser – can't stand the niggers or Jews – or actually anyone who isn't white, so the Lebanese, the Indians, the Portuguese all fall into her hate cauldron.

She learns this from her father – Herr Fleischhauer (Mr Meatchopper/Butcher) – who from knee-high has taught her skew Aryan ideals and jargon.

'Hitler had the right idea,' she'd slur-stumble out on Sunday afternoons, invariably laced with her irrationality, drunk on brandy and Coke or sour white wine. 'He was the only one who managed to restore Germany to its former glory … While the German men went off to fight in the First World War, the Jews stayed at home, made money and used and impregnated the German women!' … blahblahblah …

Wow! Why would we need to listen to tapes of Adolf when we had our precious mother as his press secretary? After slaving all morning at the stove to present her Sunday roast and veggies, invariably the subject of 'the blacks' would arise. 'The blacks are stupid. They will not be able to run this country ever. They must know their place, bloody ants. The day Verwoerd died was a sad day for this place …'

I longed for my mother to soften, to smile, to giggle and tickle me and laugh. To have her wake up one day and say: 'I am sorry – I have been wrong. I love people, no matter what colour their skins are, no matter where they come from and what or who they believe in.' But she never does.

My sister and I rebel against everything she tells us; we argue and disagree and in my childish way, I try to explain to her that the black population in our country are people too, that Hitler was a dog and a murderer.

Afternoons end in screaming nightmares, my mother slapping my sister, me trying to separate the two ... The same old same old conflict never gets resolved – it just sits and bobs, like stubborn mouldy corks on ill, algae-infested water.

I often feel as though I have been mistakenly dropped into a family where I share nothing in common with the bearer and creator of me. I wrestle with the idea that I may have been adopted or found on a street corner and picked up and taken to this home in which I now find myself. I have found out in retrospect that it's common for the addict to feel misplaced and alien and a deep sense of not belonging.

———————

So under the fast-approaching midday sun, Gail and I get drunk and giggle and cry for Bob, who's died from a gangrenous, cancer-infested toe ... We cry and cry until we laugh and laugh. '*No woman no cry*,' we slur-sing on our way back to class. We're late. No worry – it's just Miss Spinster Trophy's religious instruction class that we've been bunking on account of King Bob.

We sneak into the class when her back's turned and soon, like a modern-day Joan of Arc, all brave and upfront, I sit at my desk, chewing gum, wielding my cigarette like her vicious sword at Orleans. We're puffing away at the back, blowing the billowing smoke into the back pipe hole in the wall … We wipe our nicotine-stained lips with strawberry lipgloss and giggle our little heads off. Spliff. Splutter. Cough.

Miss Trophy's shaky scrawl is copying meaningless Bible verses onto the blackboard. No-one is paying any attention to her 'copy-these-down-class' long-suffering instructions. Instead, behind her back there is chaos.

'Look at the way she writes, she's got Parkinson's!' someone splutters.

Candy thrusts her hand up, Puff the Magic Dragoness, smoke pours out her nose. 'Ma'am,' she drawls, nasal twang twang. 'We need to talk to you about something. It's lank serious, so we really need to talk.'

Miss Martyr Trophy stops her scrawl, her back heaves an 'oh, what is it now?' huff. She waits a moment, mutters her Hail Mary's, then turns her creased brow towards us. Tired old spinster, she's got that not-a-single-joy-in-the-world-look on her face. The class waits in pounce mode, preying on the promise of the kill.

Clutching her orange honey smack-coloured beads around her never-been-touched-turkey-neck, she sighs Methuselah deep.

'Yes, what is it, Candy?'

'Ma'am, someone in the class is pregnant.'

There is audible inward breathing.

Even the boys are quiet now: are these chicks for real? Serious, or what?

'We can't tell you who she is, ma'am, but ma'am, she's having a nervous breakdown. She says she's going to kill herself, ma'am. What can we do?'

Miss Trophy writes Life Line's number on the blackboard. It is a pathetic response.

'What if she don't have a fo-o-one?' Nick the rugby captain asks. It's only 11 am and he's drunk already.

'Then she gets an aborshuuuuunnnnn!' splutters Sotoris, the Greek whose father owns the corner café.

Hyaena hysteria reigns.

Miss Trophy stoically stands her ground, weathers the onslaught storm. After all, God is on her side – that's what gets her up in the mornings, her mission to save these unruly children from a life of ignorance and damnation. The bell rings, the pack of wild dogs tumble out, desperate to escape. As Candy pushes roughly past the Trophy, her long string of beads snap off her scrawny white neck. Plink plonk they bounce all over the floor. She's on her hands and knees, trying to gather them. She's on the floor like Daddy. Down, big as a Frisco seal. No-one helps. Bata Toughees crush her fingers as we rush off to break, mad bulls to Pamplona.

On all fours, back hunched, she's left like a camel in the smoke.

I decide I'm an atheist and refuse to participate in her religious instruction class. I become obsessed with the mission to promote my own free choice crusade. It is 1982, Christian National Education reigns supreme – all schools are segregated – apartheid is in full strangle-hold force. There is no such thing as freedom of choice or constitutional rights, but I decide: Nevermind the bullshit, let me see how far I can push it. I become a disruptive force, arguing and challenging Miss Trophy on every Biblical statement she makes.

At her wits' end, close to a shaky nervous breakdown, she calls in the inspector of religious instruction of what was then known as the Transvaal, Mr Piet Stander.

Inspector Piet, I grin to myself, maybe he's like a Mr Squint-eye Colombo, and I'll salute him. I take a quick courage sip of wine out of the hip flask, as I sit in the headmaster's office awaiting my date with Herr God.

Instead a kind, gentle-looking man arrives, closes the door softly, grins wickedly at me and – tip-toeing like a little goblin – sits down. Rubbing his hands together, he says: 'So I hears youse don't want to participate in the Bible class?'

I nod, dumb statue.

Mr Piet puts his feet up on the headmaster's desk. He winks at me in subversion. He points to a chair.

'Who made this?'

'It comes from the woods, the trees,' I say.

'And who made the woods?' he asks, twinkling brown eyes.

'I'm not too sure – something called creativity. You know, creation,' I say.

'And who is responsible for this creativity or creation?'

Now the air hangs thick, he watches me closely in anticipation. Like a hungry mirror, he sees himself – secret rebel, trapped in an ill-fitting suit. He hates his goddamn job, working for the department under the De Klerk monster. He waits for my answer, like a child waits for an ice cream, sweat beading on his upper lip.

We are paused, two souls hanging in space.

The bell rings. I wait.

'A Big Bang, a force, a collision of astronomical intrigue. Who knows …? Never mind *what*. It *happened*, didn't it?'

'Good girl,' he says. 'Nice answer.'

He smiles. 'From now on, your status in the RI class is non-participation. You do not have to take part, although you have to attend. I will have this made official. Well done!'

In a puff of smoke he's gone. Dumbfounded I walk back to class, bypass the loos and have a quick Camel, hardly comprehending the sweet taste of victory, mixed with 11 g of nicotine and 1.1% tar.

Encouraged by my progress, fighting the fascist system, I decide to write a play. It's an attempt at a political drama, highlighting SA's human rights abuses. It relies heavily – in fact, all but plagiarises – Alan Paton's *Ah, But Your Land is Beautiful*. Nevertheless, it's a sincere attempt to challenge the *status quo* and its merits are in its naïve creativity.

In the second week of rehearsal, **THE PLAY IS BANNED!**

'Motherfuckers!' I scream down the corridors past the maths and English classes. The Std 6s and 7s stare from algebra psychosis, as my screams echo, my rage tearing at the walls, ripping at the dead cobwebs of compliance and deathly greyness. It is the uniformity, the nausea of it all that is the true killer.

I run and run. I know no boundaries in this zoo. Everything's set in concrete and I want to break it all up! Stir it, boil it, stir, stir, stir it all up! Projectile vomit into their faces.

A revolution was necessary to purge these fuckers. The time was now! I was a lone screamer in that sick marshmallow world of lies. Dead zombies circled me and now, like a wounded wolfet, I ran amok, howling for blood through the buzzing halls of uncreativity.

NAZIS! They were all Nazis and I was part of their Holocaust. Like sheep we walked in a line – blinded by it all. We were all part of the system, compliant. By buying bread or milk, we supported it. The rot was deep – I did not know how to stop it, stem the tide. No-one in my vicinity seemed able or even willing to step out of the sheep dip line. We were all like toy soldiers who stuck to the rules, the syllabus, endless memorandums of how to teach, what to teach, Nazi precision. Lies, lies, lies! And, God, how I hated it all!

The headmaster, Mr Cryalot, tells me he has no choice but to ban this subversive material. His hands are tied, he says – what will the other parents say? In his guidelines section 3999478884888999, he reads that no political theatre of any nature can be performed according to Christian National Education policy. Motherfuckers! Himmler whores!

Devastated, my drinking escalates. It's the only way I know to switch off and forget.

It's April '84. Final year of school – yippee, freedom is coming!

It's Wednesday afternoon and we're at my house: Gail, me and Candy. We're all drunk and giggly.

The Ouija game is neatly set out on the glass dining room table: we call it 'glassy glassy' 'cos we can't pronounce the other word. Letters of the alphabet carefully cut out of white cardboard, arranged in a circle, YES, NO, numbers 1–10.

This afternoon we have a date with the spirits.

I'm the medium of the magic circle. I like to appear spooky and weird to my friends, that's why I wear black lipstick sometimes and practise Theda Bara looks of dramatic murder in my mirror late at night.

The Bible is open on John 3:16: *'For God so loved the world that He gave His only begotten son ...'* Cool! I never open the Bible, but I read somewhere this is what you do when you call up those who've gone to the other side.

The air hangs expectantly. The overturned wine glass feels thick with promise.

'We'd like to talk to a good spirit. Are you a good spirit?' I enquire, all important.

It moves smoothly across the glass table. Y ... E ... S ...

'Can I ask something?' says Gail. I nod. Queen of the Scene gives permission.

'Who am I gonna marry?' she asks, breathlessly.

Long elastic silence, we wait, just the breathing of three restless girls. Finally:

D ... I ... O ... N ...

'Dion!!!!! Ugghhhhh – Dion Viljoen! Oh, no!!' screams Candy.

'No!' screams Gail. 'Not him. Never! Never! Ever!'

'Oh, just relax!' I hiss, glaring at the stupid, giggly girls. Diffheads! 'It may be another Dion, someone you've never met. Stop being so hysterical – Candy, it's your turn.'

'Okay,' she drawls, shaking her golden mane, like some lucky thoroughbred Barbie doll.

The boys at school love her. Long, brown, tanned legs, perky tits; her father's Dr Floyd Blueberry, anti-abortionist, he's into pro-life or something. In the last year of school, Candy falls pregnant, not sure who the daddy is, like all good daughters of anti-abortionist crackpots tend to do.

'Well, whatever he's into, he's fucking ugly,' says razor-sharp Gail.

I look at her sharply. The bitch is reading my mind again.

'Who is?' asks Candy, ever bright blonde.

'Dion Viljoen,' Gail says Cancerian slick; the crab grins wickedly at me.

'Your turn, Candy,' I say, gritting my teeth.

'Ummmmm … ' Finger in the mouth, dumb Barbie is gathering attention. 'Ummmmmmm … Let's see, what shall I ask?'

'Anything, ask anything. What colour your fucking toothbrush is,' I hiss.

'What am I gonna be?' she shudders seductively.

Bravo bravo fucking bravo!

Her long curtain of blonde gold waterfall hair shivers. The glass creaks slowly.

M … U … T … H …

'What's that? There's no such thing!' Candy's small-voiced squeak.

'Wait!' shouts Gail.

… E … R …

'MUTHER!!! It says you're going to be a mutherrrr!' laugh-screeches little crafty crab.

'It can't spell well,' I say, defensively gleeful.

'This is crap,' says Candy.

'Look, if you're going to insult the spirits, you may as well fuck off,' I snarl.

'What am I going to be when I grow up?' the smooth crab interjects.

D … A … N … C … E … R …

Quickly, gracefully decisive, it obliges, grinding glass on glass, creaking its truths out in the stinging afternoon of suburban unbliss.

All eyes fix on Gail, smug little crab-pig, slim dancer bitch basking in the evil orange of the dying light.

My turn at last!

'What am I going to be?'

Hoarse plea, waiting for the word 'actress', biting lip, tasting blood metal.

The glass swells in its silence. Pregnant. Heavingly overdue.

Seems like hours we pause. Days, years pass.

Finally:

H ... E

   ...R ...

O...

    I ...

       ... N

A ... D ...

      D ... I

     ...

... C ... T ...

'It says "heroin addict",' smile behind her glassy eyes, Gail announces to the world.

'What's that?'

I'm pale, fists clenched, knuckles grinding on the glass-topped table.

Suddenly the glass starts flying across the table to all letters, faster and faster. Glass is swinging to and fro, to and fro, to and fro, screeching scratch on glass.

Then, from nowhere, the black cat is on the table, wild-eyed, low-pitched growl in the throat, like some miniature black wild panther. I turn the glass over, burning hot.

I want them to go home. Fuck off, oh please, just fuck off.

They oblige, white and shaken, wordless zombies.

I dash off to my cupboard the moment the front gate closes. Find the packet of pink and white marshmallows shoplifted earlier. Stuff them in my dry mouth, chew chew chew. I binge, mad pirate on my treasure loot.

Glassy eyes staring ahead, hand to mouth, mechanical doll. Little Alice in Nowonderland – swallow, swallow, swallow.

Tummy distended balloon cannot hold anymore.

I hug the toilet bowl, my cistern lover, my life comes gushing up, too fresh for bile, the Styrofoam marshies won't sink. Damn them, damn them, down, down, down.

I hear the hoot of Motherbitch, she expects me to open the gate.

Plan B:

Bury the stubborn little fuckers, my mother is hooting and I must hurry to get rid of this evidence before me. I thrust my hands in the cistern water, gather the floating pink and white Styrofoam, shove them in a plastic packet. Down to the bottom of the garden. With my hands like a bone-obsessed puppy, I dig a crude grave, hide and bury the evidence of my shame.

Again I hear the hoot of Motherbitch.

Open the gate yourself! I rush back in. I lie on my bed, heart racing. My biology book stares blankly back at me; meiosis and mitosis, alibi for my stray thoughts. I glare at my watch – two hours from supper-time.

Supper-time was something else. Since I can remember, my mother's culinary skills entailed repeating the same meals week by week, over and over again.

Monday – meatloaf.

Tuesday – spaghetti.

Wednesday – chops.

Thursday – bangers and mash.

Friday – fish.

Saturday – hamburgers.

Sunday – roast.

That's why, I tell myself, I bring it all up, to get at her for her boring cooking.

When Motherbitch found out, it killed her inside. She could not show me love and whatever little she could give she put on a plate in the form of a meal. And here I was, taking it all (and more), stuffing it down and puking it all up again. What an ungrateful, bad girl! It cut her to the core like piano wire through a newborn's skin. But, instead of talking and reaching out, attempting to fix the rot that seethed beneath, her response was to hide the bathroom key hoping that would defeat Brendabulimia.

Motherbitch never looked at anything full on. Instead she hid her head, ostrich widow, and chose the task of motherhood to martyr her life with. She made a pact with death to hold its candle for the daddy who had jumped ship, and widow whittle her life away. Motherbitch made us pay, as only one so disappointed by life can.

CHAPTER 5

BRENDABULIMIA

The disease of self-hatred first surfaced in 1981. Me 14 and in a line to be weighed by the gym teacher, Miss Slimenough.

Like sheep getting dipped or being slugged for Mad Cow's disease, at our Auschwitz delousing, we await our weigh-in at the scales. It's my turn now.

70 ... 71 ... the arrow shudders and settles. I nearly die peeping through half-shut eyes.

'You should lose some weight,' the little 48 kg flyweight teacher grins.

In the loo, I stuff my face with a chocolate, holding my disgusting blob tummy and swear to go on diet.

I find *The Beverly Hills Diet* in the local stationery shop that afternoon and shoplift it. It's written by an 'I'll-answer-all-your-prayers' American, Judy Mazel.

Fruit and popcorn are the recommended staple food. It's a six-week miracle cure for all that blobby fat and unsightly, flabby cellulite.

Like my new Bible, I follow it perfectly. I do it once, I do it twice, I do it three times over – and the weight sheds off me like a snaky skin. I lose 21 kg in three months. The results are miraculous. I lie on my stomach in the bath: I balance on my sharp, new-found hip bones, like a slim little seal, to and fro, to and fro, I rock myself. Reed-thin have I become. No longer one of the boys and everyone's buddy, I'm suddenly part of a meat parade, one of the girls, in the middle of the thick of things.

I am so happppppyyyyyyyyyy!!!!
I am so hungreeeeeeeeeee!!!!!

So I eatandeatandeatandeatandeatandeatandeatandeata ndeatandeatandeatandeatandeatandeatandeatandeata ndeatandeatandeatandeatandeatandeatandeatandeat.

I am starving, I need to eat. But I can't get fat again, no! Never! Not ever! Then, quite by chance, I discover a wonderful way to have my cake and eat it, so to speak. I begin to eat as much as I want and then straight away I head for the loo, drink a litre of water and – whoops! It all comes up. Miraculous! Bingepurgebingepurgebinge.

I manage to keep the weight off, but I become completely, absolutely addicted and obsessed with food. I can't control my hunger and the emptiness inside grows and grows. I find myself wandering down supermarket aisles, clutching bars of chocolates, doughnuts, marshmallows, anything sweet and yucky. Most of the time I manage to eat a whole lot in the shop before filling my blazer pockets with as much as won't bulge out and look too suspicious. Like a bank robber, I case joints for my food fix. Afterwards, I bring it all up in public toilets – when my stomach's crammed full and too distended to keep it all in.

In moments of cold clarity, I feel deeply revolted and shamed by my out-of-control behaviour. Here I am puking up all of this food and my fellow South Africans, the black people, are starving, being tortured, and killed. And me, whitey bitch – spoilt, sick, selfish, stupid little pig – am puking my life away, enacting my middle-class neurosis. The sight of myself in the bathroom mirror as I come up from the bowl for air, eyes streaming, makes me vomit all the more.

Less than two years later, 1983, I'm sitting in Tara, the city mental hospital.

My mother has found out about Brendabulimia. She takes the bathroom door key and hides it. I no longer have a private haven; she can walk in on me anytime she likes. We go into the shrink's office. Devastated, oh how disappointed, my mother weeps for the entire hour.

The shrink is an anaemic, bespectacled blimp. I lie and test her. We leave. Heavy silence hangs between us. Swollen, rotting grapes. The entire journey home my mother sniffs and silences me out, like Frances Farmer's mother, hurt, raw red, pathetically wounded.

As I watch the trees blur by on Jan Smuts Avenue, I wonder what Miss Beverly Hills Diet, Judy Mazel, is doing … how I wish she was my mother. (Some years later, it's reported that Miz Mazel is found in a hotel room stuffing chickens down her throat. I heard she's dead, shame, poor Miss

America. Wonder how many of her devotees ended up like me, shoving their fingers down their throat.)

That night after Tara, I dream my puke is trapped in the geyser, built in the ceiling above my bed. The ceiling starts bulging, swelling like the pregnant belly of a dirty orca whale. The paint heaves and sighs, its birth pangs more incessant. Too heavy, it bursts down all over me, the sickly sour of vomit, years of it, cascades and covers me in a puke tomb of lumpy, sick, sour afterbirth. I am buried and flailing. My body, my face stringed and stenched out, in stringy mucous sick... I'm awake in sleep, watching myself watching myself – dreaming.

I awake. I'm out of breath.

———————

Which gets me to Noddy.

I don't think she's breathing at all.

It's nearly 10 years later and we're at Boy 2's flat in Hopkins Street, Yeoville. It's me, Boy 2 and Lenny, the lizard boy, dumb, aggravating, infuriating Lenny. Quart of Black Label forever stuck to his left hand like some kind of new accessory, he shuffles around like an ancient park bench alkie.

He's come over to pick up tabs of Rohypnol that Noddy's organised for him and Boy 2. They've already popped one each and now I wish he'd go home so that me and Boy 2 can go upstairs and fuck ... although that's probably not going to happen because these damn downer pills make my boyfriend so relaxed that getting sex together is the furthest thing from his mind. I start rolling a *skyf*.

I have picked up a serious dope habit from student days spent at UCT from '85–'88. I spend most of my time at Michaelis Drama School, stoned out of my mind, boycotting lectures and hurling stones at cops in student protests against the fascist government. It's the height of the State of Emergency in our apartheid-ravaged land and the call to voice our disgust against the state feeds into all my 'rebel looking for a cause' tendencies. Sometimes I forget why I am protesting 'cos I'm just too stoned. Anyway, I want to be an actress, and actresses can do just about anything and get away with it. Dagga encourages memory loss and feeds my imagination, plus it makes the whole unsavoury campus scene a lot more palatable.

Now it's June, early '90s, winter-pale African sun shines a soft blurred light. Everything snails on slow. I've smoked about seven joints today.

Noddy is lolled asleep in a corner; her tongue is starting to slop out of her mouth. She gives me the creeps. I hate downers, losers. I mean, what's so great about popping a pill that makes you fall asleep all over the place?

I've never taken any sleeping pills. I'm into life – I go to gym five times a week. I smoke dope – but, hey, who doesn't? – and it comes from the earth, gives me lots of energy and makes me laugh! Not like these somnambulists I see before me.

Unscintillating company forces me to watch CNN playing solo solo in the corner. Special report on the AWB's failed coup attempt in Bophuthatswana. Stupid, stupid Dutchmen who went and fell on their bigoted bums in Bop, while their great leader, die *Moses van die mense*, Eugene the Queen Terreblanche, watched it on TV, from his Joshua Doore lounge suite, brandy and Coke in right hand, Gunston Plain in the other. He falls asleep as the TV shows the khaki-clad idiots trying to re-enact some crazy, long-gone Boer dream of seizing Mafikeng from *die terroriste*. But they get shot right in front of us, in our living rooms. They die on TV, while Eugene snores.

It feels like the country's fucked. Bombs have been going off in the big city. Pliff plaff people dying, maimed bits of legs hanging on windscreen wipers, everywhere you go you feel it, the terror. The stinging air is violin-taut in tension – today is the day that maybe they're gonna get me. Pliff plaff. Life is cheap here.

With the negotiations around the first ever democratic election now over, after such a long time, it feels like the boil is bursting, pus oozing down the jacaranda-lined streets, the highways and byways. The country teeters on the brink of civil war, unsteady stiletto, unsettled settlers. Everyone's drinking and taking something, to cope, trying to get away from it all.

ONE SETTLER, ONE BULLET screams from graffitied ghetto walls on Tudhope Road, Berea. The world stands back at a nasty, safe distance. Where is Uncle America, John Wayne and Ken the Barbie when you need them?

———

Noddy is a Barbie doll – barbiturates: Seconal, Rohypnol, Sepental – but her real love is Wellconal. Pinks.

Once a month she drops by with a script of downers for Boy 2 and Lenny.

'Artists need sleeping pills.' Lenny glares at me, as my boyfriend pays for the drugs. Lenny hates me; he knows what I'm thinking.

'I'm a genius, you know,' he says, glowering at me.

Yeah, right.

Lenny is King Bumrat, living off people like Boy 2. Suckers! But the real twister is that he insults anyone who offers him their stupid generosity. I'm not taken in one inch by him.

Unlike most druggies, Noddy is not a bum. She never asks for money ever. But one day she stumbles into our flat and, embarrassed, asks Boy 2 if she can borrow R50 for pinks.

That night she falls asleep on the couch. We throw a blanket over her and go upstairs to sleep. In the morning I wake to hear the kettle whistling on and on downstairs. I stumble into the kitchen to see Noddy's head stuck to the boiling kettle. She is fast asleep.

Two weeks later she's dead – blood clot in the groin, her favourite shooting place. Everything packs in; body at 27 has had enough.

'She still owed me R50,' says Boy 2, distracted tear in his left eye, as he pops a pill she left behind.

––––––––––––

It's early evening when Lenny comes over with a sample of the music he's composing for Boy 2's film that later wins us a passage to Europe. Ah! Behold our 'genius of the world' egomaniac muso, who writes two bars of a stolen John Cage sequence, samples it over and over and calls it a 'masterpiece'. I'm helping my boyfriend make it and Lenny's just an intrusion.

I tell him about Noddy. He ignores me. 'Where are the bevvies?' he interrogates Boy 2 and heads for the fridge.

'There aren't any,' I say. 'Why don't you bring your own, for a change?'

'What kind of people are you?' he says. 'How do you expect me to work when there are no beers? In fact, how am I supposed to create when there isn't even a line of fucking coke? What kind of movie is this, anyway? It's a joke! Fucking amateurshhhh!' he slurs. He breaks a plate as he helps himself to the leftovers of last night's dinner.

I am raging as I leave the room and suddenly it's as clear as day what my next move should be. I come back quietly into the candle-lit kitchen, I sigh heavily. I approach him, all conspiratorial-like.

'Okay, Lenny, we know you're right, so ... we've decided to give you something.'

Now he's all ears, interested.

Out from behind my back I produce a mirror, bankrolled note, and the hugest line of cocaine, snaking brilliant white in a long, thick line.

Lenny nearly passes out in glee. Little Rumpelstiltskin, he grabs the bank note, lurches forward and like a manic

Electrolux, snorts. In a second, the line is completely vacuumed up.

Without as much as a ta, he's off missioning to the Harbour Café on Rockey Street to bum a beer. What he doesn't know is that the so-called heap of cocaine is in fact Eno's, an effervescent for upset tummies. That's what he deserves, King Bumrat.

I grin to myself as I imagine the foam bubbling from his burnt-out nasal membrane. Later I saunter down to Rockey Street, hoping to survey my handiwork … I see Lenny passed out in a corner next to the pool table. I prod him with my pool cue. He's dead to the world … that's Eno's for you!

Rockey Street is where everyone congregates, it's the early '90s and the one place in Jozi where white and black people mix and it feels semi-normal. The rest of SA seems still to be living in an ox wagon. I met Boy 2 on Rockey Street in 1992. A few months earlier I had narrowly escaped getting married to my 'fiancé', Boy 1, by sleeping with his best friend. (Oh, how grown-up and goddamn awful the word 'fiancé' sounded – think that's what really put me off!) Altogether, it had not seemed like a nice day for a white wedding.

I was running an alternative theatre, Voltaire, on the corner of Rockey and Raymond streets, where every Sunday night we'd put together a programme that ranged from strippers to fire-eaters, to noisy garage bands, to plays, to movies … It was our attempt to subvert the current *status quo*, to say 'fuck you' to the oppressive vibe of the apartheid government. People flocked in droves to the joint, to have a laugh and get carried away.

The line-up that night was a preaching parrot, a stripping nun, an ambidextrous prostitute and a singing virgin. We tried to show a South African film every week. Encourage our motley culture, local-like. That night a nine-minute anarchic local film was to be screened.

I didn't know the film-maker, but I'd seen the movie at a club one night and I remembered a part of the film where a guy ate his own shit and I thought it was hilarious. (That guy, in fact, turned out to be Lenny. How prophetic!)

I was intrigued by the one who'd made this piece of celluloid – I mean, who would seriously make someone eat their own turd on the big screen? At Voltaire ours was a 1 m x 1.5 m and our projector an old, rickety 16 mm rented from the porn shop downtown.

Late that afternoon, before the show, I arrive to meet the film-maker to thread his film and give it a test start. I am used to waiting for artists who are always late, but I'm surprised to find a grey-haired, beautiful, pale-faced, artistic-looking guy with the most perfect nose I've ever seen, reading a newspaper, waiting for me! Wow! African time must be taking on a new meaning...

Upstairs we approach the ancient-looking film projector with trepidation. We're both pretty non-mechanical and we keep showing the film backwards. We get on seamlessly. After an hour of non-success with the projector, we climb out the window of the theatre and sit on the roof and smoke a lovely Swazi joint.

The sun is setting on Rocky Street; we are a storey above everything, kings of the Black Sun. It feels surreal, like we're tripping on good acid. Ecstasy. I think perhaps it's there, we fall in love. I'd like to kiss him, but I don't because there's work to do.

Next up for the rehearsal is the singing virgin, a blonde Pamela Anderson look-alike from *dit lyk vir my 'n snor is meer nodig as 'n tjor* city Pretoria.

She has a backing tape of Gloria Gaynor's *I Will Survive* and Shirley Bassey's *Diamonds are Forever* that keeps running ahead of her and on the side line, an over-ambitious mother who keeps freaking out.

Later that night at Voltaire, in true Dadaist fashion, chaos reigns supreme. The place is packed, sweating and bulging at the seams. Sunae the singer is dressed in a brown suede cowboy suit; like a mangy mule, she kicks the evening off. As predicted from the dress rehearsal, the tape starts running ahead of her. She is visibly panicking and the audience – hyaena dogs – start baying for blood.

A riot breaks out. This is like Alfred Jarry's theatre. *Ubu Roi!* Far-out!

From the sound and lighting board, I watch the chaos with intense glee, my hands are sweaty. There are 120 people crammed into a venue designed for 60 max. Never mind a fire hazard – I recoil in huge mammoth pain as I'm shocked by a faulty electric current on the board. It sends a volt right through me. I look up and the grey-haired guy is staring at me. I shiver with anticipation. We grin at each other, secret code to whatever. Shock/volt/Voltaire, this must be meant to be.

Later, I take him back out onto the roof overlooking Rockey Street. This time we kiss. The stars shoot in the black night sky. He moves in instantly. He becomes Boy 2.

CHAPTER 6

SLAVE TIME

'I am going to cut you up in little fucking pieces and throw you on a rubbish heap.' Boy 2 is holding a mean claw knife to my neck, we're parked on a backstreet and withdrawing and manic from too much crack, and now we have no money and we need some smack to come down.

'Get out of the fucking car, go and suck cock ... I don't give a fuck what you do, but get some cash!'

'I can't, I can't, you can't force me to -' I snivel.

DWACKKK! Oh, yeah! He takes a leather cosh and hits me on the back of the head – instant knob on the brain. Stars shoot out my vision. I touch my matty scalp and look at my blood red fingers.

Oh God, he's going to kill me ...

The drugs were turning Boy 2 into a monster and I was as monstrous in my own pathetic, screeching, whingey way ... The more addicted I got, the more helpless I got and the more I seemed to push his motherfucker buttons ...

Withdrawing brought out the worst in us, sad slaves on the road to nowhere ...

I didn't drive, had never driven. Years before, when I was 19, I had decided that 'the more you drive, the less intelligent you are' – something I had heard an old homeless man in the Alex Cox movie, *Repo Man*, say. I had held onto this innocuous statement like some precious, God-inspired mantra.

A slave to the shit, I was powerless and completely beholden to Boy 2 for his car. I needed him to get my drugs or to drive me to the dealer and take me back. Sometimes I thought that was the only reason I stayed with him, especially when he was on a psycho mission. Like a dumb slave, I was getting more and more scared of and dependent on Master Mad Dog by the day.

Being a slave in the 14-15-16-17-1800s couldn't have been much fun. Stacked sardines in human sweaty faeces. Being a slave in the 1990s was like cold, curdly vomit for dessert.

Waking up – sweaty skins, aching bones, runny nose, stretching sinew in smutty bed.

So you withdraw, take five days off, arrange a cover so no-one will know. Visit a good doctor, who understands and gives a script.

Get:

Methadone, sleeping pills, muscle relaxants.

Armed with the miracles of modern medicine, we lie down to death.

Smutty sheets, nightmares, writhing. Torture, drawn and quartered, Middle Ages torment, legs ripped off, limbless torsos.

Go on vacation. That seems like a plan – a good move. Withdraw.

We go on endless 'holidays' to try and get off the stuff. Scenic places become static postcard backgrounds, nonchalantly watching our nightmare. Nature is scary. Extreme beauty can inspire feelings of extreme sadness.

Withdrawing can be done anywhere, but no matter what, you're gonna have a shit time. *'Everybody cries,'* croons Michael, *'sometimes.'* He tells us to hold on.

So you do, you hold onto your insides as you kneel and puke. You seek a comfort zone, a nest of salt, weeping, weeping, weeping. Feels like everything's dripping out – like big, open sores. Begging for something to deliver you from this evil – this-this- grasping, gasping, going down – then:

'I've got to have a hit! Just one, please! Give me a fucking hit! No! Fuck you, fuck you, give me a fucking hit! Did you hear me!? Fuck you fuck you fuck you. GIVE ME A FUCKING HIT!!!!!!'

Bash! A cosh to my head again! I had always wondered how a woman could stay after a man hit her: now I knew. You just don't go when there's nothing to run to. And not driving gives you even less choice.

I'm pregnant!
Oh, my God!

It is on a day of snivelling noses and sweaty skins that we buy a home pregnancy test on the way back from the 'Brow from scoring. I'm a week late and I've been freaking Boy 2 out, neurosing about the possibility of pregnancy.

My hands shakily open the wrapper and I drip, drip three little drops of urine, saved in a bottle earlier, from my first morning wee, into the window of the little plastic kit. We watch the two blue lines appear. I know for sure that the outcome will be positive. I just know. I have never taken the test, I have never been pregnant, but I know this time that I am. Those blue lines feel like a life sentence. We both fight back the tears; the silence in the car aches and smothers us. Years seem to pass ... two junkie children overwhelmed by the enormity of it all.

'Oh, my God,' I think. 'Now I am going to have to stop using drugs.'

———————————

I know when it happened – the exact moment, in fact! Three weeks back we went on one of our jolly holidays, to a mountain resort outside Jo'burg, to once again – for the 180th time – withdraw and get away from the city and the dealers who we so easily blame as the source of all our problems. We believe, in typical junkie style, that it's all everybody else's fault, that if we are not around the shit, we will miraculously have the desire to use, lifted.

The place is ironically called Utopia. As soon as we arrive, we put all the lights out in the little wooden chalet, take a handful of sleeping pills and lie down as the mosquitoes arrive in droves to feast on our heroin blood. The rain begins to fall and doesn't stop for the whole weekend. Our supplies, packets of ready-made food from Woolies, lie untouched.

We have no appetite. We are two weak lepers. Ticks and spiders join the mosquitoes and binge on the untouched food and our bare body offerings as we lie like sick statues and sweat away the hours.

On the second night, into our 30th hour of withdrawal, Boy 2 becomes horny and needs to get it on with me. In fact, it could be with anyone – but, hey, it's *my* body that shivers beside him.

For the past year we have been using condoms as contraception and now they are downstairs. In a daze, I push him away and crawl on all fours to the stairs that lead to the lower floor. But, drugged out on Rohypnol and blinded like a bat in the dark, I miss my footing and fall down the wooden stairs, bashing my head on the edge of wood.

I give up on Mission Condom and crawl back between the sweaty sheets, rubbing my aching forehead lump. Not really sure what happens, but next thing he has it in me and it's all over in that erection-for-20-seconds-thrust that happens during the withdrawal process. I fall asleep. In that moment sperm meets egg, greets her and says: 'How about it? Let's make some joy …'

Conception takes place. I'd always hoped for a more romantic, more intentional one.

My friend Sav the Starman says that conception occurs when a spirit/soul or being circles around the two people who are engaged in the sexual act. A vortex is created and the being hovers with the 'mother' over the next nine months, while she grows the shell inside her … Just before birth, the soul enters through the fontanel and decides whether to stick it out with her as its host. Sometimes it leaves and that's when a stillbirth, miscarriage or cot death occurs.

I suppose abortion is a whole other story. The option of termination never comes up with us. It's as though seeing that test result, we just know there's no turning back. At first, we walk around in a daze and tell no-one. We go and score to help ease the shock. We smoke and barely look or talk to each other. There is something so scary, so permanent that is happening here ...

The knowledge that a thing was growing inside me and that it would one day be a whole human being terrified me to the core. I knew that I would never be alone and wild and free again. I knew that everything was about to change and, worst of all, I knew I would have to stop drugging – I went into extreme panic attack mode.

Having seen David Lynch's film *Eraserhead* six times in my life (it is, after all, one of my top five movies ever), that skinless, yowling head of the freak baby in the shoebox begins to haunt me. I imagine I am growing an alien extra-terrestrial, one-eyed monster inside me. It is twice the size of me and its father! Then my dream changes into a blonde-haired McCauley Caulkin look-alike, who's inside a child tent with me and Boy 2 and is ordering us around to cook and clean and do whatever is his whim. Oh, my God, it's either Eraserhead or McCauley – can't decide which one's worse ...

'Maybe this baby is going to be the one that saves me.' Liam sings something similar in the background. I weep and weep, there seems to be no feeling of Happy Event, no Oasis, no Wonderwall at all.

Yet deep inside I am hoping that the pregnancy is going to get me to stop using and that at last Boy 2 and I will have an incentive to clean up our act, become decent human beings, get the picket fence thing going and live happily ever after. Didn't all people do that when faced with imminent parenthood?

THE WEDDING

'Hey, little sister, what have you done ...?' Billy Idol thought it was a nice day for a white wedding – I don't.

I am three-and-a-half months pregnant when Boy 2 and I are shotgunned off in the Catholic Church in Klerksdorp. On finding out I'm pregnant, his family, who reside in this scintillating North West town, plan a quick one and I – like the extra carriage – feel shunted into it. I don't even inform my family of the exact date. I buy a brown and black little mini-pinafore, put on black stockings and 18-hole Doc Martens, dark maroon nail polish and matching lipstick ... I look like a little pregnant Goth ...

In the car from Jo'burg to Klerksdorp, we smoke a rock and have a few chases of smack to even it out and when we get to the church, everyone is waiting.

'Let's have another hit,' I hiss at Boy 2.

'Don't be fucking insane!' he says. This is probably one of the least romantic marriages this planet has ever witnessed.

We drag ourselves into the church and after the service, which goes past me in a drugged-out haze, as the priest is looking for a pen for us to sign the papers, I nudge Boy 2 and try to get the bag of heroin off him, so I can go for a quick chase in the toilet.

He elbows me and hisses once again at me to shut the fuck up. We sign our union, both aching to get our grubby paws on the shit. Ah, for a hit now, to ward off the imminent feeling of sweat and withdrawal … The reception is mainly his family affair, there are no happy speeches, no joyful toasts at this event – it's as though everyone senses that the bride and groom are walking down the aisle of gloom.

Next morning we head back to Jo'burg, back to the dealer. It's as though nothing in the universe has changed in any way …

Instead of a honeymoon to an exotic Indian Ocean island, the following day I find myself at the doctor. Having made promises to Boy 2 now for nearly three months to reduce, stop, minimise, cut down, I have not been able to stop using the drugs at all. I have been putting this appointment off for weeks, because I know when I go, I will probably have to tell the doctor what is really going on and get some help.

CHAPTER 7

THE HONEYMOON/REHAB

Tripping up the stairs to the Melville Clinic, the day after the wedding, on a wintry blustery day, the little hump is growing in my stomach and I feel like bringing up. This is no feeling of morning sickness. No case of honeymoon newly-wed nerves. It is a far more sinister nausea that is gripping me and squeezing me from the inside.

The world glares at me inside the waiting room – like everyone can see I am a bad, bad junkie who is putting her unborn baby into jeopardy. At reception, they ask me my name. I am married now ... since yesterday, I don't know what to call myself.

'Mrs Junkie,' I say under my breath. Boy 2 butts in, takes over. I wander off. Sit down. Wait.

Boy 2 is pale; he tries to pat my back to reassure me. I want none of it. I just want a hit. My name is called. I don't recognise it.

Staring at the scan, my throat dries into a desert as the doctor points at the shape of the little alien on the screen. 'It's a boy,' he says. Oh, my God, this is too damn real.

'Is he OK?' Boy 2 manages to get it out, hoarse whisper.

'Of course he's OK,' says the doc. 'Why shouldn't he be?'

The time is now. I know that I will have to say the unsayable.

'I have a problem ...' I whisper.

'What's that?' asks the good doctor.

'I am ... I have ...' I bite my lip, draw blood, the metal taste gives me courage. 'The problem – I – I can't stop using drugs ...' There! It's out.

The good doctor is silent as he folds up his stethoscope.

'I have – I have been ... using heroin – a bit of crack. I can't stop.'

Oh, God, it feels like my chest is being hammered open, I am drowning. Heartbeat is drumming deaf into my tympanic membrane. Get me out! I am so ashamed. I want to run.

'You need to go into rehab,' he says, worried. It's immediate. Do not wait, do not pass 'Begin', do not collect R200. 'Go home, pack some clothes, go in today. Go now.'

I nod. We leave. I weep in the car.

'Please can we just go one more time?' I beg Boy 2. 'Please, please, please ... I will go straight after. I just really need a hit. Please. I promise.'

I beg him, my Master Fate Decider, my driver, my line to the love of my life, my everything, for I am nothing. I beg my husband like a blinded bitch at a robot with a begging bowl. I beg enough.

So off we go.

———————————

All my bags are packed, but I'm not ready to go.

We're sitting outside the rehab in the car and that damn tune 'Leaving on a Jet Plane' is playing like some wailing wind-up cat on the radio. It won't leave me and how I hate that song … it's so stupid, so soppy, so '60s.

I am a stone concrete statue. I can't move to get my things out the boot and walk through the doors. *You do not do you do not do any more black shoe.*

I bend down out of eyeshot and have another chase. I watch as the brown, runny, gooey heroin makes a little snake down the foil. I imbibe the pungent cloud like it's the last bit of oxygen left on this dying planet.

'C'mon, that's enough now,' Boy 2 says. He's had it with me.

'Oh, it's OK for *you* – you're going to just sit smoking and get fucked while I have to suffer inside … I don't wanna go now, please, I'll go tomorrow, please, you can't make me!' I weep in a heap.

He gets out the car, picks up my bags and begins walking towards the entrance. I sit and stare ahead. Dumb little Alice in Wonderland … Then my feet move forward … Automated, I walk to my noose. My jailer husband walks ahead. Oh, God, how I hate him!

Rehabilitation in this country is for the privileged and wealthy few: it costs a fortune – on average R15–30 000 for four to six weeks' treatment – which is really weird, if you come to think of it – because by the time a junkie is ready to get some kind of help, we have no means to pay for our recovery ... Because we've smoked, spiked, snorted and drunk all our damn money.

I use R2 000 from my already in-the-red overdraft to make a down payment. This one's a state-subsidised rehab – it still costs R10 000. I'll deal with that problem later. And all I can think about is what this cash in my Levi's pocket could have bought me: I make endless mental calculations: R2 000 divided by R50 (cost of a rock/bag of brown) = 40 units of drugs – and now here I am willingly paying to get locked up and screwed in the head!

It's the end of May 1996 and Jo'burg's winter has set in and is blowing icy cold ... the wind bites at my fingers and ears. I walk in past a group of patients sitting in the lounge. My black woollen dress shows the growing outline of the baby, I feel their eyes bore into me, in their Pontius Pilate judgment of the new arrival.

Like Bad Mary hobbling off to Bethlehem, I move on to the infirmary, where Sister Betty, a Jamaican nurse with a funny wig, does her thing on me. Her hands are icy as she feels my distended belly, swelling stretching skin. 'It's very small,' she accuses, her voice even icier.

She takes away my razor, lighter and cash. I glare at her. 'So I can't even shave my legs?' 'No, you are correct. You can't,' she says freezing me out. She sounds like Bob Marley's horrible cousin from Reijkavik.

Checked and weighed again like an Auschwitz sheep, I am shown into the detox room, dosed with Methadone and tablets. For the next 72 hours I pass out into oblivion, waking up every few hours to try and eat some of the cardboard meal that always seems to be waiting for me, cold on a platter.

I sweat and dream and lose all sense of time and action, of who I am and what I feel and what I am doing in this place where the wind blows through every crack. It screeches into the night, while Boy 2 drives up and down, down from Westdene, up to Hillbrow, getting cracked and smacked, so high. This rehab is just off a major road that carries loads of traffic downtown and to Hillbrow. If I listen very carefully, I swear I can almost hear his car brake and gear-change just outside my window.

Motherfucker!!!

On the fourth day, like Lady Lazarus, I arise from my bed, weak and depleted – but the withdrawal fever, thank God, is over. I shuffle to the lounge and there I meet my fellow inmate addicts. Over the next few weeks I get to know them, like a shell-shocked family who've suddenly just found out they're all related.

THE REHAB CAST

First there was **Johnny:** A Portuguese hottie, crack addict-*cum*-dealer, tattoos, good body. He fascinates with a story of how he'd lock his screaming girlfriend in the boot of the car when they scored. If she made a noise, he'd keep her there for hours. Finally he'd let her out, put his beloved pitbull right next to her at the table and then she'd have to watch as he smoked. If she as much as moved her left finger, the pitbull had instructions to go for her throat. Drugs, I s'pose, make people behave in very strange ways. Without crack coursing though his veins, he was a sweet Catholic dude trying to be a Muslim.

Joe: 40-something – a long-haired, ex-music industry cokehead who'd blown over R3-million on drugs, women and partying. According to his elaborate and rather far-fetched war stories, he'd even smoked up an aeroplane. He was on the run from some bad deal in the 'Brow and the rehab seemed to be his hide-out. Penniless, he was now seemingly very willing and dedicated to getting straight. He bugged me with his Jesus Bible-bashing and let's-all-get-clean ra-ra talk.

Telkomtjaart: A typical Afrikaner who worked for the national phone company and who'd picked up a serious crack habit on the side. While installing a phone in a house in Sandton, he had been bust robbing the place to pay for his drugs, when the owners came back unexpectedly.

Instead of firing him, the phone company had graciously paid for his rehab.

Mo: The little Muslim wise man who always had his fez on, said his prayers three times a day, facing east and displayed the serenity which I think that rehab prayer was talking about. He was kind and always had a wise word when he saw me ... he was managing to convert Johnny to Allah.

Elzabet: An overweight Afrikaans girl from a little one-horse town called Heilbron, she came into rehab with a serious heroin addiction – a gram a day and a sackful of chips on her shoulder. Only 25, she had lost three babies in her life and seemed to latch onto the imminence of mine with strange obsessiveness. She gave me the creeps – had that possibility of being a maniac with Munchausen's syndrome by proxy: you know, the one where you hurt people while you pretend you are helping them. Every time she saw me, she would weep and tell me how when she was 18, she had fallen pregnant. Her mother, on finding out, had arranged abortion tablets from a doctor, given them to her daughter without her knowledge and put three black plastic dustbin liners on her child's bed. Elzabet had bled and aborted profusely while her mother lay in the adjoining room on her lilac bedspread, reading the Bible.

Cora: A 14-year-old blonde butter-wouldn't-melt-in-my-mouth number, she was a serious heroin, crack and pinks addict. Every morning she'd make me tea and stroke my hump. She slept most of the time and was always late for sessions, at which she'd arrive rubbing her eyes and nod off again halfway. It seemed like she was really escaping her depressive life in dreamland.

Dr Sandra: She was never seen without curlers in her hair. A blonde 40-something doctor who had been struck off the role because she was a Pethidine addict and had done some botched-up job on a patient. She pranced around the rehab place like her prince was about to come and sweep her away in a four-by-four pick-up truck.

Naseeba: Also 14, she was the rudest girl there by far, and I really liked her. She was very bright, very cheeky and very angry. She was in the house for a serious crack, dagga and buttons (Mandrax) addiction. From a wealthy coloured family, she was in rehab much against her will. She had the latest gadgets, the best designer label clothes – but when visiting hours came, no-one arrived to see her ... When Boy 2, who never missed a session, visited me, we would watch her all dressed up, staring at the gate, hoping that she would get a visitor. In the end I would invite her to sit with me and my hubby and pretend he'd come to visit the both of us. At the end of visiting sessions, she would rant and rave and run amok, exhausting and irritating the rest of the house. I understood her like she was me and knew all that rage was just about not getting enough love.

Camilla Cruella Deville: I knew she hated me from the moment her emaciated, hollow eyes glared at me from across the room. Huddled on a couch, scowling from a smoky haze of a 40-a-day Craven A habit, she watched me after I got out of detox, walk through the lounge, overladen with books and chocolates, duvets, blankets and flowers that Boy 2 had brought to give me as a semblance of creature comforts.

She had spent most of her teenage years hooking and could often be found staring from her window at the distant shape of the Hillbrow Tower and Ponte building, as though her soul was longing to get back. She had a serious intravenous downers habit, mainly pinks and smack, and she hated everyone and everything.

'Gimme a smoke,' she snarls at me as I try to edge past her. She takes a long, deep drag, her eyes narrow. 'My baby died. Cot death. And I wasn't even using drugs.' She stares at me and my tummy accusingly.

I look down, cough and light a fag.

'How can you take drugs and be pregnant?' she lashes a low blow.

My eyes prick with the threat of hot tears spilling. Fuck her! Who is this scrawny little slutty bitch?

'Well, that's why I'm here … I'm trying to stop,' my hoarse whisper hardly breaks the accusing silence of her glare.

Then Johnny struts in. It's midwinter, but he's wearing a tiny, tight black vest showing off his newly-found, rehab-exercised, bulging muscles, and tight black jeans. His fez from

Mo snuggles neatly on his newly-shaven scalp. I'm wrapped in three of Boy 2's jerseys and tights and leggings.

'Hey, chick, you wanna come and play some volleyball – get some sun?' I nod. 'You a little bit pale, hey,' he squeezes my cheek affectionately. I immediately feel at home with him and follow him out like a grateful bleating sheep, relieved to be out of the Cruella gripping glare.

'What's *her* story?' I ask him.

'Oh, fuck her, she's just a sour *poes*,' he laughs.

The midwinter morning sun all but blinds me. I'm weak from withdrawal and scared and skinny and I long to be back with Boy 2 in the comfort of heroin heaven, and not with this sick bunch of weirdos.

We play a bit of volleyball. Naseeba joins in, but I'm seriously weak and miss most of the balls that sail over to my side. Instead, I sit on the edge and smoke another fag. Joe bounces in, he's been training like Johnny in the make-shift gym and they all look so damn healthy and enthusiastic, they almost bring a bout of my vomiting on.

We drink bad rehab coffee/gravy powder and they ask me my story. Reluctantly, I tell them about the smack and crack – I underplay everything. They all beam and hug me and tell me I'm doing the right thing for me and the baby and they will help me with whatever I need. I feel like saying: 'With whatever I need? You mean you can score some shit for me?'

The main thing, they say, is that I'm doing something about my problem. I smile and nod, but inside my addict voice says: 'What problem? Babe, you don't have a problem.

Look at them! These people are losers! You're just a little nervous and scared 'cos you're having a baby, but you know you can control it, you know you don't really have to be here. It's Boy 2 who's the addict, not you – case of mistaken identity, babe!'

I like that voice – it feels so familiar, like the only reasonable one in the whole joint.

Meal times make me feel like I'm on some loony Christian cult farm. Before eating, we hold hands and they say things like: *'God grant me the serenity to accept the things I cannot change, courage to change the things I can and the wisdom to know the difference.'* Then everyone swings their hands together like ring-a-ring-a-rosy circle in playschool, and they chant: *'It works if you work it, so work it – you're worth it.'*

Oh, God, I hate that part, it drives me wild! We all look like a bunch of fucking sheep!!!

The Olympics are on and I steal as many hours as I can and lounge on the couch between counselling sessions, staring glassy-eyed at the screen as fit, able-bodied people run around, throw javelins and do active, energetic things.

The feeling of health ever returning to my ravage-racked body seems like a far-off impossibility.

There is a rule that you can't watch TV during the week, besides the news, so I of course make sure I watch at every opportunity. I keep getting blue letters for my transgressions. I tear them up. That's what I'm really struggling with, these damn fucking house rules! If you watch a video, it's got to be on the weekend and no drugs and no sex in the content!

I mean, come on! That excludes almost every flipping movie ever made!

You can't use the phone, and this one really killed me. Boy 2 was my last connection to the real world and I needed to speak to him at least twice a day: he was the closest thing I had to a shot of smack. And so I, who'd just got married, would shout and scream: 'I'm pregnant!!! I need to speak to my husband! *I need to I need to I need to!!!!*' Until I got my way.

For any transgression we committed, we were given pink or blue letters describing our crime, like we were in detention at some sad motherfucking school. No wonder on an almost daily level, people were talking about Jumping The Wall. 'JTW' meant scaling the high wall encircling the property, getting over onto Main Road, Melville, then onto King's Way, hitching a lift and escaping to Hillbrow to score, of course. By car, it was about a 10-minute distance to the possibility of smacky cracky heaven ... Our drug-addicted minds fantasised about this journey hourly.

Jumping the wall was a capital offence in rehab: immediate expulsion. But, hey, who gave a fuck, 'cos if you were over the wall, they could expel you all they liked – you were gone!!! It was also called RHTing – Refusing Hospital Treatment ... well, hello, du-u-uh! Of course I would be gladly fucking RHTing!! But although I thought about it, I never seriously made plans to use or escape the joint.

Cruella did.

One night, sick of everyone and everything, in the dead of darkness, she scales the 12-foot wall and soon picks up a lift into the 'Brow, her skinny frame shivering in anticipation at the thought of meeting with the love of her life – the pinks. On Soper Road she does a quick blow job for a sweating German tourist, and a hurried hand job for a bad lieutenant, which gets her R100. With her syringe and pinks stashed safely in her grey bitty panties, she's back in the house before you can say 'RHT'. None of us even know that she's gone. We're all sleeping, me dreaming of being smacked.

We wake up and she's not there.

Word soon has it that at 3 am Sister Betty found her stone cold, syringe in the neck, blood eking into a sad red puddle. She's dead on discovery. No recovery. The body has already been taken away by the time we awake. So, although I never get to have a good time with her, her image stays with me for years. They say this disease is progressive. Three years later when I myself am Soper-Roading my skinny body, I catch a reflection of myself in a passing car window. The eyes that stare back at me are hers.

CHAPTER 8

GETTING OUT

Was one of the hardest things I ever did. The life I returned to when Boy 2 picked me up outside the rehab, on an ice-bitten morning two months later, had not changed in any way. In fact, it had gotten much worse. The cobwebs of crack and smack had just gotten tighter and more unruly.

While I was inside, Boy 2 had been using like some mad, snorting dragon. I knew that he wasn't okay because each time he'd come to visit me, he'd look more wild-eyed, skinny and unkempt.

Sometimes he forgot to wipe the brown heroin marks off his front teeth and when he smiled he looked like a homeless maniac, not a nice boy from an upper-class family, with a doctor for a daddy.

When the counsellors asked me whether he was an addict, I'd lie and cover up and say: 'No, he isn't using, he's actually fine. He's the one who takes care of me; it's **me** with the problem.'

I'm sure they took one look at him and knew that the bruised-eyed, skeletal-looking guy who wore a rippy military jacket and seemed skittishly on the edge was obviously a junkie. But when you're using and strung out of your mind, looking for ways and means to get your next hit, you don't think anyone can see it.

My lie about him not having a problem made a change, because up until now, on our three-year drug journey, I had always been the one in the outside world who played the 'I am fine, responsible and together' role.

From that first hit we'd had in '93, at Matt's Yeoville den, Boy 2 had known he was going to have a problem with the smack. He loved the feeling of numbing out, the womb-tomb effect – and so, naturally, heroin fulfilled his deepest umbilical desires. Usually filled with fear in the real world, he found that smack took away his anxiety, neurosis and fear of flying. Of falling.

As soon as he realised how much he loved the drug, he tried to give it up, bargain with it, cut down, abstain for days ... He sensed the dark pull of it and because of his deep-seated, self-preservatory nature, he began to play cat-and-mouse. Except that Boy 2 somehow always ended up being the mouse ... poor squeaking, shivering little wretch who always got mauled and clawed in the end ...

I, on the other hand, went straight into 'No, I am bigger than this, I don't need this stuff, I'm just having fun – I am definitely not addicted' mode. Perhaps I knew that if I were honest about my love and need for it, and admitted its hold on me, I might have to stop taking it – and the thought of stopping terrified me: abstention was for nuns, and was definitely not part of my Bigger Plan.

I was not the first one to go to rehab: at the end of the previous year, Boy 2 had broken down and confessed to his family he was a heroin addict. I played the good, caring girlfriend, wringing my hands and talking in low, concerned tones, to his sisters and mother in the 'oh, look how supportive I am!' cover-up. In some way, I think I actually truly believed in the role I was adopting. (I'd not gone to drama school and perfected the Stanislavski method for nothing.)

So I'd go with his glamorous, bejewelled mother in her enormous white BMW to visit him in a rich rehab just outside Jo'burg north. There we'd sit and look at his pale and shaky withdrawal face, his mother and I bonded in concern. Truth was, a few hours earlier I had caught a taxi into 'Browtown, picked up three bags of brown and three rocks. Driving home I'd feel like a hugely famous rock star, being driven by my chauffeur, my heart racing at the thought of my imminent inhalation fest of heady narcotics. At home in the cottage we were renting in the back garden of Boy 2's sister's house, I would lay the gear out in front of me, put on some cool, raspy Nirvana and slowly begin an hour of drug intake.

Kurt sang about being happy because he'd found his friends in his head.

He felt ugly, but that was okay, ' *'cos so are you ...'*

I was in solo drug heaven – doing as I pleased without Mr Meany Man trying to control and dictate every move I made, and squeeze me for every breath I took.

Returning from visits to him in rehab, I would make sure that I had stashed a third of my haul so I would have something to smoke on the return home. I never for a moment thought that perhaps it was I who needed to be in rehab, getting help. No, I was simply FINE, as I breathed in the heady, intoxicating smoke that buried me deeper into a sweet cocoon of denial.

Playing Miss Healthy/Good Girlfriend while stoned out of my brain was a mind-fuck. Deep inside I knew I was lying and as the lies grew, the fear grew with them. Those fat, wriggling little maggots buried deep in my veins, in the very core of me, swept away my fear, ate up the little 'real' that was left in me, and they called their new home-hovel 'denial'. I suppose that's what it all boils down to in the whole recovery scenario: the depth of the denial determines how difficult or easy it is for an addict to get real and get clean.

Looking back, it's no wonder Boy 2 got clean in early 1999, a full six months earlier than I did … I suppose my disease was just a little more cunning and divisive and ordered me to do a whole lot more research before the deck hit my face.

———

So I spent 24/7 of the two-and-a-half months in rehab in a Fort Knox of reservation and denial. Each time I went into counselling sessions, I would nod at the right time, know when to say the right thing and mouth all those clichés that I thought they expected of me: 'My life's been such a mess till now!'; 'Everything's clear at last!'; 'I will definitely come for counselling when I leave'; 'I know all I have to do is stay clean'.

But inside, my addict voice was operating overtime. I'd stare at my shrink Hugo and the voice would be a cacophony of hisses: 'Look at this wanker, what does he know about using drugs!? ... Oh, **please!** Do you **really** believe I'm never going to be able to have a drink or even a teeny little joint again! ... Do you want what this prick's got? Wanker!'

But I do recall, one particular day, getting entirely uncomfortable when Hugo sat me down, looked really hard at me and said: 'Do you know what it's going to be like when this baby is born? Do you know how your life is going to change and how challenging things are going to be? The baby is going to scream and cry, and you are probably not going to know what to do, and the baby will keep crying, on and on ...

'You are going to have days when you feel like you want to tear your hair out and go out and score and escape everything. I am worried about you because I don't think you have the first idea of what you are about to get yourself into.'

I remember staring at the floor, his mouth moving in my blurry side view, a wave of noise thundering in, like a good rush on poppers, trying to silence the penetrating fear that those words evoked in me.

'I'll be fine. I've read lots of books,' I lied. 'I don't feel nervous at all. Umm ... I need to go to the loo, are we finished?'

The baby was growing – I could feel him. He was like a really active grasshopper kicking at my stomach. Nurse Betty called him 'our little soccer player'. I was about six-and-a-half months pregnant now. I had been eating and sleeping in rehab and the baby had benefited – he was right on track. Sometimes late at night I would put the lamp on and watch his little elbows making bumpy waves against the distended skin on my tummy hump. My inmates regularly gathered round me, hands on my tummy; sometimes it felt as if my unborn child knitted us broken little misfits together. But late at night, when the world was quiet and I had a rare real and honest moment, I would all but choke to death on the pure and absolute terror of it all.

―――――――

In rehab, they tried to teach us how to handle this terror and stress – to conquer our fears. The sessions were called 'stress management'. One of the counsellors would arrange a whole lot of drugs on a table: crack, smack, pills, joints rolled up (rather badly) and some beers. Then she would start a confrontation session, get a bit hectic with us – try to push our buttons and see how we'd react. It was actually pretty pathetic, because it was an unreal and simulated situation. We'd all sit there, fists clenched, staring at the drugs as if we were watching a Formula 1 race, on and on, in circles. Of course, none of us grabbed the shit ... except for Naseeba, who – without fail, every session – lurched for a Mandrax pill, a joint and a rock and headed off for the corner, smoking greedily and happily like a little pig in the mud. She just didn't give a fuck and I admired her for her audacious courage.

All the while we watched her enviously, trying to be detached and healthy, when all we wanted to do was bury our nostrils and tongues in it, and gobble all the shit.

The counsellor would stare stoically at us, not 'interfering with the process'. I don't think they ever really bargained on any of us actually **using** the drugs when they concocted this hare-brained idea ... so Naseeba's gluttonous tactics forced them to rethink theirs.

It didn't take me long to figure out that rehab for me had just been a break between two hits ...

On leaving, I stayed clean for exactly two hours and 48 minutes.

———————————

Unpacking my clothes back in the Westdene house, I had to navigate my way around the mess that had piled up during my absence. Not that I was ever a clean Pollyanna, but 60 days of Boy 2 in bachelor junkie mode, with absolutely no cleaning, had left the place in a stale-smoke, mouldy *Little House on the Prairie* nightmare.

When I walked into the bathroom and saw Boy 2 hovering over a piece of crumply aluminium foil, trying to smoke under the basin so I would not see him and be tempted, I flipped my little oh-so-deprived, depraved and craving lid.

Lurching forward, I all but grabbed the foil and orange BIC lighter from his smack-stained hands.

'What the fuck -?' he yelled, caught off guard.

'I want some gimme some gimme gimme gimme some!!!!'

He held it above his six-foot frame, making it an impossible task for me to get to it.

'*Motherfuc-c-cker-r-rr*!' I screeched. Oh, God, here we were starting back at square one.

We both knew it.

'This is stress management … it's good for you,' he said. Dog. Sadist. Fucker.

'This is what they tried to teach you inside. You've got to be able to cope staying clean in all types of situations.'

Yeah, right.

Five minutes later I had persuaded him to take me on a drive through the 'Brow – just to see if it 'still looked the same'.

Twenty minutes later, I had my head below car window level, parked in a crummy side-street alleyway, smoking hungrily like an infant desperate for her mother's milky breasts. Oh, God! How I had missed it! Like the return of a lover, gone for many months, I slithered yearning arms outstretched towards it. How wonderful that first heady dissolve into Nirvana was … I was back in love again … Then, on the car radio, Kurt came on and sang all crackly:

'*She eyes me like a Pisces when I am weak,*
I've been locked inside your heart-shaped box for a week,
I've been drawn into your magnet tar-pit trap …

I wish I could eat your cancer when you turn black …'
Nothing in the world could have been more perfect … It was me, the brown and the velvet, static, smoky voice of Kurt Cobain … it was truly Underground.

When Kurt *'Come as You Are, As a Friend, As a Known Enemy'* Donald Cobain died on 5 April 1994, 22 days before our Great First General Election, we'd been doing smack for about a year.

'Here we are, now entertain us!' sang Kurt, roughly angelic – and over 10 million people smelt the Teen Spirit, bought the record and joined in the Nirvana pilgrimage.

Everything about Kurt felt like I was meeting the boy part of myself. He was pushing boundaries, both personally and creatively, and I loved and respected him for that. In 1986 he formed Nirvana, a band that was to set the world music scene ablaze a few years later with a new, edgy brand of music: grunge. Kurt was always a little bewildered and 'rabbits in the headlights' with all the success that came his way … 'If there was a rock star 101 course, I'd really like to take it,' he once observed.

In order to handle those pressures and an aching stomach from a childhood ailment, Kurt found heroin and began smacking in the early '90s. So when I came face to face with the brown, it was only natural I should follow suit.

And if anyone made me feel like leaping on my fire steed and hunting and chasing that big old dragon, it was Kurt.

BLOW-OUT

When Kurt blew his brains out with his shotgun on the Persian rug in his Seattle home in April '94, we were devastated, left reeling barbels on a tugging fishing line – as if a brother/sister/lover had died. The radio and TV splutter sick odes to our king. Meaningless words bounce off into the marshmallow nothingness of outer space, satellite dishes serve nothing.

The hole hangs open all day in my hollowed heroin heart. I walk around, numb zombie, crashing into walls, a dumb nurse unable to fix my cavernous heart. We're left rudderless, as if our captain has jumped ship. The king is dead ...

Conflicting reports abound on the television: Kurt's alive, Kurt's dead, Kurt killed Courtney, and Francis then turned the Uzi on himself and 64 people who were wanking in a park. He was murdered when Courtney tried to get the stash off him. Evan Dando, Courtney's new squeeze from the Lemonheads shot him.

The media fodder chomp on the chewing gum of misinformation like a slathering bulldog at the bit. That Kurt is dead is all that matters and gives me an excuse to hit the biggest rock and smoke the longest line of smack – I wanna speedball down this horror highway to hell. I wanna die and be with Kurt! My sorrow books into the heroin hotel of my scab-sheeted mind.

I think of his wife, poor Courtney, demented she-witch baying her billowing rage. Everyone blames Miz Love. **'May all the Nancy Spungens rot in hell!! Ruthless**

psychopath vampire slut! Courtney killed our angel Kurt!'

Somehow I know in the same shoes, she could be me – I could be her. I'm also the bad girlfriend slag heroin bitch who later becomes the bad, doing-drugs, non-caring mother bitch …

She's so easy to blame, with her bleached white peroxide princess look, purple angry tracks on white spotty arms and that skewed, sluttish 'I've just given you a great dirty blow job' mouth.

She is everyone's controversial scapegoat throw-stones-at girl. Smoking and spiking in her pregnancy the previous year, she announces, this way, she will experience 'less pain, smaller baby, easier labour'.

I, too, am appalled at her candid callousness. 'How absolutely disgusting!' I think with the rest of the world, only to later find myself in the same sick pea-green boat.

It's so easy to blame Miss Love for all of Mr Cobain's problems. Maybe she was dangerous, co-dependent and all that and more, but so would most people be when crucified by the hoglights of relentless pressures, judgments and pig paparazzi.

Maybe they were too young, too rich, too quickly.

Maybe poor Courtney in reality was trying to fight for her life, for **his** life, to help get him off the stuff when she, like me, was trying to act as if she was much better than she really was. Weeks before his death she was part of a tough love plan to shake him out of his heroin slumber – who knows if that sent him over the edge? Seems like everyone thought they knew what Kurt needed.

'We should have let him have his numbness!' screams the grieving she-witch widow at the Seattle candlelight vigil.

Courtney is burnt at the stake. The paparazzi pig dogs, like ebola apes, leap lyrically, waltzing to the tune of their tabloid lies. Sperm in their eyes, bloodshot.

But beneath her brashness I am sure that Courtney aches like we ache.

No smack will assuage the deluge of pain. He leaves us with a chilling legacy of self-mutilation, the cruel consequence of heroin gluttony. We are Kurt's sacrificial gouging goats. He is the hero lost, he is the father I never had ... he is the disappearing man, the twin of every man I have ever loved – the unavailable, the non-present, the dying, the bleeding – all slip-sliding away from me.

I hit and spike and cut myself up in honour of them all. I feel so sad.

───────────

Back in the car in the alleyway, three hours out of rehab, Kurt sings and crackles static, immortal.

'Hey! Wait! I got a new complaint.'

I feel the baby kick in time to Nirvana.

CHAPTER 9

BIRTH

'Don't PUUU-U-USS-SHH-HHH!!!!!!'

Four women are at the base of the hospital bed, crowded around me, my legs splayed open, inspecting my dilated vagina … it's 3 am. I have been in labour since 9 am the previous day – it's going on for 16 hours now and I think I am going to die!

I have just been administered Pethidine. I chose not to have an epidural when it was offered hours ago 'cos 'I want to have a natural birth', I tell the midwife earlier. Natural birth! What a laugh! I have been hiding in little hospital corners at the end of *The Shining*-like corridors all day and all night, smoking heroin – and now I want a natural birth! The pain of contractions is unbearable. I feel as though I am being ripped and torn – blown apart … they decide to give me the Pethidine hoping I'll go to sleep, as I am the only woman yelling in this hospital …

Because of lack of funds and some way-out idea of having a baby in a 'people's' hospital, I have chosen to give birth in the Coronationville Hospital in Westbury, a renowned gangsta crack-land suburb … '*Tupac lives!*' is graffitied on the surrounding wall, which is encased in razor wire and looks more like a prison than a place for the sick, the birthing and dying. I am also the only white woman here, and I definitely think I prove the theory that white people's pain threshold is much lower than that of people of colour. I banshee-screech into the night. Earlier, before I was wheeled into the birthing ward, yashmaked Muslim women lay stoically beside me, like concrete bricks, not a whisper from their clam-shut mouths.

Now the screaming has subsided and the combination of heroin and Pethidine has made me into a grog dog ... lost in a fog much like what I suspect death may one day feel like. I can hardly breathe, let alone push! But my body, despite the drug cocktail, knows it needs to get this baby out ...

Boy 2 stands at the foot of the bed – he is pale-faced from a too-much-crack/smack 24-hour binge and maniacal worry. The helpless, hand-wringing husband, like in a Jane Austen novel, he clutches my hand. I lacerate his palm, pushing my nails deeper and deeper into his pale flesh ... He is a crucifixion. A thorn in my side.

'Jesus, fuck! I am going to die!' I hiss, imploring him with my eyes.

'Just breathe,' he says, unconvincingly ... I draw blood in his palm.

I move between hysteria and comatose delirium, my muscles seem to be doing a thing on their own ... I can't control any of this! I am falling asleep, I'm drowning ...

They have tied a foetal monitor belt around my swollen belly and are observing the baby's heartbeat on a screen, but the belt is far too tight and between the pain of contractions and the strangulation of my midriff, it feels as though I am going into a deep panic attack.

'Get this fucking thing off me!' I am yelling. It is devouring me, like a psychotic cobra. The midwife and sisters join forces, sinister bitches, and hold me down, clawing my frantic fingers off the belt.

'Please, can I squat? Please, I can't lie here … I'm dying!' I implore my jailers to set me free, it feels like I am going to go in-fucking-sane … 'I can't do this lying on my back … Pleeeeze!'

I feel like a Mengele experiment. Blank eyes stare back. They gather in a whispered huddle. The conspiracy deepens – it bleeds down the hospital halls, onto the street, across the black sky night, into outer space … my screams rebound.

No-one's taking notes.

Finally, back from deep debate. 'The baby will fall on its head if you squat,' says Mrs Einstein Midwife.

'Fucking bullshitt-t-tt!!' I scream. '*Lots* of women squat, people do it all the time!! You should know – you're black! What about all those books that say "steer your own birth, be master of your destiny – squat!"? That's what I read; that's what Oprah says!! They *all* fucking say you can squat!!' But this is deep, dark Africa – it's a holocaust hospital, my pleas dingbat on the walls, nonchalant in their symmetry.

Suddenly my breath falters, shudders, all but stops. An oxygen mask is shoved on … oh, God, we are all going down.

"'Gas! Gas! Quick boys!" An ecstasy of fumbling, fitting the clumsy helmets just in time ... but someone still was yelling out and stumbling. And floundering like a man in fire or lime ...'
Wilfred Owen, British World War I poet, Standard 7, Roosevelt High ... I can't get these words out of my head ... I am going to die ... like Wilfred.

Cold steel hacks at the rim of my vagina. Snip snip snip.

'It's blunt,' says the midwife. She gets another pair of scissors to hatch job me. Oh NNNNNNNNNOO-OOO-OOOOO-OO-O-O-OOOOO!!!! Imminent mutilation!! I push with an almighty strength that comes from somewhere else – not here.

The baby is born 10 minutes later.

We call him Joy.

I peek a look, for fear of a misshapen monster before me. He is perfect – a slippery, bloody eel. He scores 10/10 on the Apgar score (heart rate, breathing, muscle tone, response to stimulation and colour).

STITCH TIME

If I think it's over, the worst by far is yet to come ... The Butcher Bitch of Coronationville begins to stitch my episiotomy wound. She holds a huge thick needle, she injects my perineum and begins to sew my flesh ... it is indescribable, the pain that ensues ... At last the psycho sewer has a white bitch beneath her – it feels like she is making me pay for every apartheid sin that was ever committed. And then she casually misses her mark and pushes the needle stabber into my clitoris.

'FUCKFUCKFUCKFUCKFUCKFUCK!!!!!!!!!!!!!!! That was my *clit*!!!'

'What do you think you're doing?' shouts Boy 2. 'Are you giving her a fucking cliterectomy? I thought they only did this in West Africa!'

'Somaliaaaaaaaaaaaa!' I shout.

I'm on a quiz show, the weakest link by far, but alas – there are no prizes!

Back to work, deadpan she stitches me up and leaves without a word. Baby is brought in. I don't want to know. I am passing out; he's put on my breast. I sleep as he suckles ...

I'm woken up three hours later. It's 7 am. 'You're being discharged.'

I can hardly focus. 'Please. Please let me sleep.'

'We need the bed. You must go now. Your baby is down the corridor in the incubator.'

Baby? Oh, God, I have a baby! Oh what to do, what to do!?

I stumble out of bed, big heavy cow in a shapeless nightgown; I bend to pull my 18-inch Doc Martens on. As I straighten up, a river of hot blood rushes out, streaking down my legs. 'I need to wash, bath, clean this –' I point to the unimpressed nurse. She huffs and points me down the hall.

Blindly I walk, collide with a trolley full of placentas ... liver-like bleeding hubs of maroon and red dripping afterbirth, the nausea rises. I gag. Push into the toilet area. More blood – it's everywhere, like a serial killer came in and did the whole ward … I look at the mirror: oh, God, I look like Stephen King's Carrie. Two rural Zulu girls, teenagers, stand naked except for beads around the waist at the washbasins trying to scrub more blood. Mudpacks cover their faces. I am tempted to ask them where they got the treatment.

I find a call box.

'You've got to come and get me,' I weep to Boy 2, who is back at home consuming more shit. 'I can't be here … the baby needs to sleep a little,' I lie. 'I really need a hit, I really really do.' I put all my best of desperation into the handset. Like my fairy godmother, he arrives within 10 minutes.

We pass the ward where Joy is under ultra-violets in an incubator. He looks perfectly alien to me. Perfectly fine, but perfectly alien to me. Like a bad traitor, I leave him there, promising to be back within three hours. I really need to score, smoke something. I feel like my cunt's been ravaged by 300 pitbulls. I take a quick glance at the baby as we leave. In three hours' time my single status will be changed forever. In three hours' time I am going to have to become a mother, but right now … I am going to get high!!

———————

The baby is six weeks old.

We are not coping; we are groping like two blind bats in the dark, holed up in the wedding present house we have been given, in Westdene. We lock the door. We unplug the phone, no need to – it's been cut off – paid the last bill five months back.

Switch on CNN full-time.

Our little bundle of Joy is at home, suckling 24/7 on my milk and heroin honey-laden breasts, smack/milk milkshakes.

I know he is addicted – I can't bear this thought, so I switch off – in typical junkie style. I am the mother and I am the dealer-feeder-killer. What to do? I know if he is deprived, he will turn into a red ball of screaming heroin withdrawal, yet as he drinks, he becomes more dependent. I find it hard to look at the truth – feeding my son the milk of death. I'm so weary and sore from birth, episiotomy stitches still aching tight in my ravaged cunt. I'm too weak to resist him; his hungry little rosebud suckling mouth finds me, everywhere, latches on my too-full breasts. He sucks into contented dreamland as I chase the dragon on a torn-up piece of tin foil.

My baby bat is so calm, so serene … he is a pleasure to behold.

SST (Sick Side Thought): all babies should be given this shit, then there would be no screaming, no yowling noise – just the delicious tomb of dreamy silence.

His deep black eyes, little olives, stare ahead; he watches the entire three hours of Kubrick's *2001: A Space Odyssey*. The foetal-like whale sounds of the astronaut entrance him. We, me and Boy 2, no more than babies ourselves, hold hands in umbilical union. We watch him – parental pride glows. Our son – our Joy-Boy. We cannot see the truth of this picture. We are too smacked.

We do everything together, we bath, dress, comfort him. We're latched like gooey jelly to each other in a co-dependent nightmare.

He fits in with our junkie nocturnal routines … A junkie, like a vampire, loves the dark … He sleeps when we do, 3 am – wakes when we do, 11 am. He is always there strapped in his baby chair … watching us from his throne on our vampire missions, sucking our way to Hillbrow hotels and back to heroin hell home. He is the Prince of Egypt, we bow to him, we worship him as we suck on crack pipes, drown in the ether of smack.

I need to start getting him off my tits. I am tortured by the knowledge of what I am impinging on my son. We buy milk formula. Slowly I begin to wean him off my tainted milk. Every third feed, then every second, and so it goes – until six weeks later he's only drinking from the bottle and my heavy breasts begin to dry up. His transition from smack to milk is seemingly seamless. We smack on. My guilt is appeased.

We never have any food in the house. Any cash is spent on smack and foil and crack and lighters. Sometimes we don't even have the R4 or R5 for a lighter – then we use matches and twist toilet paper tightly into a semi-wick and light the pipe for the rocks or chase the smack, with these burning tissue smouldering makeshift lights. It's sad, pathetic, when R4 seems like a fortune!

Boy 2 is starving. I catch him late one night with the tin of baby formula: he's stuffing spoonfuls in his mouth.

'What the fuck do you think you're doing!?' I screech at him, grabbing the tin of yellow powder.

The formula is dry and he can hardly garble a word ...

'You can't eat the baby's food!' I yell. 'We don't have cash to buy him more. Leave it alone!!!'

Things are falling apart.

The doorbell batteries have been taken out. Even if people ring, we are oblivious now, we are burying ourselves deeper and deeper, curtains drawn on our catatonia cocoon.

I hear my mother calling and calling from the other side of the high wall. We sit dead still. We wish to see no-one ...

WORKING

Somehow, at this stage, we manage to keep working. If you can call it that. Sitting in the edit suites on the third floor of SA's national broadcaster, the SABC. We work late at night when no-one's around. Like cat burglars, we patter through the corridors ... I imagine rivers of blood gushing down from one end to the other, like in Kubrick's *The Shining* ... While I attempt to edit, string sequences of shots together, Boy 2 phones the Nigers in Hillbrow, organising complicated pick-up plans. Our Joy-Boy stares from his little portable car seat. He is taken everywhere with us. No nursery sweet little Tinkerbell routine for him ... He watches our every move. Transfixed by the flickering buttons of the edit machines, the on/off /in/out flashing signs, the squeal of tape on fast rewind ... by four weeks old our son is an ace editor.

We have been commissioned to make a 30-minute doccie on one of SA's most successful film producers. In normal circumstances, he would be a great network connection to make, spending time with him ... finding out how he ticks ... but our curiosity for our work has long flown out the window; our drugging is top priority – everything else seems like a cruel intrusion.

We smoke over half of our R60 000 budget ... blow it on the crack sizzle and pop of rocks. It runs down in thick brown gooey heroin syrup as we sniff, snort and smoke like bad, mad dragons and get smacked ...

The producer resides in Durban, the headquarters for his company. We decide to score R1 000 worth of drugs the night before we leave for the Durban shoot. Our baby is to stay with my sister.

Before the night is through, we smoke everything up, our entire shoot stash withers away in smoke ... now we must make plans for another grand to get some more shit, so we won't be sniffing and crying while we're shooting the celluloid king.

Four hours into the shoot in Durban, clammy dirty tropical city, our noses begin to run. 'Let's go get some stuff,' I whisper to Boy 2, who is sweating as he lugs the huge, ungainly Betacam from one spot to another. The king of celluloid answers our semi-conscious unfocused questions, we look entirely disinterested, his irritation is obvious. We don't care about anything. All we can think of is a hit, anything to alleviate the impinging withdrawal.

Somehow we manage to see the day through, but by 4 pm we know there is no overnight, no hotel/motel/Holiday Inn stay in this coastal town ... 'Let's go to Point Road – that's where the hookers are,' 'I suggest. 'I'm sure we can find some smack there.' Boy 2 refuses. He is in murderous mode and I am feeling the ensuing fear that his rage and withdrawal bring on ...

Not driving, I am like an unwelcome parcel, sniffing and whinging, waiting to be taken from one spot to another ... As usual, the journey will be in his hands ... he revs the car up, squeals the tyres and begins the long trek back to Hillbrow.

He dials a number. 'Papa, it's me. I need one and one ... please have it ready for me, my brother ... I'll be there in ... five-and-a-half hours. Meet me in the parking lot ... Yes, of course I have the cash.'

I close my eyes ... I know we have no money, but when we get there we can deal with it ... Later, later ... everything these days is always justified by a put-off. Right now I need to take a hike from this reality of crawling, sweaty, screaming skin. I close my eyes. I know there is the relief somewhere out there. *'Somewhere over the rainbow bluebirds sing, somewhere ...'*

CRIME TIME

There is only one option for the addict when the funds dry up, when the cheques have bounced, when all friends or acquaintances have been begged from, with those lies:

'Umm, we need R50 for nappies for our baby …'; 'We need medicine …'; 'We need food …' Oh, pathetic pretenders.

Of course, once the cash is in hand, all pledging promises become empty straw pieces. It's straight to Little Lagos. The beast reigns supreme. He is us. Morality and consciences flew out the window way back, when the addict monster moved in.

A junkie called Darryl hooks up with us. He is a skinny, Twiggy-looking dude with huge bushbaby eyes. He's spiking. He's a hard-core junkie. Like an Arctic explorer, I want to push boundaries – I think I want to try the needle, and he's my way in.

One afternoon we have no money and Darryl and I decide to leave Boy 2 behind and head off for a clothing store in the northern suburbs. We make a quick, ridiculous plan before we enter. I will walk in and begin to shake and fake an epileptic fit. Of course, the security guards will all rush to attend to me while Darryl fills his sports bag with shoes. He'll give me a sign when ready and we'll meet at the car. *Trés* simple.

Everything goes as planned. Within six minutes of entering, I am lying frothing on the floor and a huge, hulking, boerewors-like security guard is sending radio signals to emergency vehicles. I see Darryl wave at me – he's ready to leave. I jump up and say: 'Don't worry. I feel much better,' and run outside to join him in the car. We are delirious with excitement.

'Fuck! That really worked!' I cackle gleefully.

On Soper Road we stop and throw the shoes out on the pavement. The Nigerians swarm like a bunch of hungry Biblical locusts.

'Hang on!' one shouts. 'There are only singles here, there are no pairs – where's the other shoe?' He holds up a gorgeous leather shoe in disgust.

Oh, God – Darryl has stolen all the left shoes and forgotten the right ones behind. How fucking stupid! Of course no-one wants one shoe. They all move off, muttering in disgust. We finally beg a R20 bag of H off someone and Darryl heads for the chemist to buy a syringe. After all that stress, I can feel that today is the day I am going to spike. We enter the Westdene house and Darryl begins to prepare his fix.

Boy 2 walks in.

'If you do that, if you let that needle anywhere near your arm,' he glares at me, 'you can fuck off right now. I will never talk to you again. Do you understand!?' He storms out.

It's weird how, in the midst of this aberrant situation, a protective, soft side of Boy 2 emerged. Over the next few years, even in the darkest and deadliest corridors of our existence, he never stopped trying to protect me. Perhaps he actually loved me and I loved him too. In the end, I always listened to him.

I look at Darryl and the blue vein that I have been working on, pulsing through my white sun-deprived skin. I shrug to my shoe-stealing mate, get up and follow Boy 2. I never spike.

The shoe incident puts me off that type of silly petty theft. I know there are better ways to get cash!

I find my niche in life: discover I am an ace forger. I can copy any signature, photograph it in my mind and then reproduce each curve, each squiggle, each line to perfection.

We are editing our piece on the famous producer at an outside company. I stumble on a cupboard one day while looking for a black fine-liner and I see a stack of cheque books, unused. They stare at me. They wink and flirt and do little groin grooves, hip squiggles, they call me closer. I come.

I tear a clean cheque, from the middle, really carefully; I wipe my fingerprints off the cover. On the way out I pick up a returned cheque and now I have a copy of the three signatories.

I begin stealing, one a day. One a day amounts to many by the end of the month. By the middle I am grabbing at handfuls … I get home and practise for hours. It reminds me of Nicholson in *The Shining*: All work and no play makes Jack a dull boy … I write my 'names' over and over again – it's almost meditational. I am good!

I decide to write cheques for under a grand. It seems less suspicious; I don't think banks query those … I'm shocked at how simple it is and how my hand flows and reproduces them perfectly. Maybe I could work for the CIA, I think as I espy my work, my Van Gogh masterpiece.

Boy 2 goes into the banks, I write the cheques. We have a sweet oiled system going, we are real Bonnie and Clydes, real Natural Born Killers: oh, how exciting this is ...

But try as we might, there never is enough: the cheques run out like a hungry, unplugged drain. The cash finishes ... the need is like a never-ending long dark monster hole that yawns, bigger and bigger, gets wider and greedier, needing more and more to fill its yowling belly.

At 6 am one morning, having smoked through the night, we go for 'one more' trip ... There's always 'one more' – never enough. Our 'cheque stash' has finished hours ago and now we have no cash. But this is not unusual – we always somehow manage to manipulate the Nigers, who swarm about the Mountbatten Hotel entrance, with false promises and dreams of elusive payments ...

At the bottom of Nugget Hill, an almost 90-degree skateboarder's dream slant, the car runs out of fuel. Joy is strapped in the baby seat behind; he's been eyeing us with his all-knowing olive eyes for most of the night.

Cursing, Boy 2 ditches all efforts of starting the vehicle and marches ahead on a solo mission, dragging himself towards the top of the hill.

I watch for a while, then realise that unless I follow suit, I am not going to get the smallest whiff of a hit. So I unstrap the baby, put him on my hip and stagger forward. I feel like I am chasing the bad, naughty Pied Piper of Hillbrow. I must get me to the top lest the rats close in. I curse Boy 2 under my breath: how can a husband leave his wife and child in such a predicament!?

Whenever I am really angry with Boy 2, I refer to him as my husband. My husband ... What a sick dream this is! This is not the way it's meant to be ... there should be a picket fence, a green lawn and dinner on the table ... he should be coming in from the office, hanging up his hat and calling 'Hi, honey, I'm home!' – and I should emerge from the Hoovered kitchen, pretty and aproned, and kiss my grey-suited hubby as he tries to guess from the aroma wafting from the oven what's for dinner. Look, see my home-sewn oven gloves!

How can it all have turned to this sour, pea-green mockery? I want to cry, but my tears are acid, my face is hardened, my throat is constricted, my jaw is concrete in my cold addict's face.

It seems to take forever before I finally huff and puff myself into the cockroach-infested foyer of the hotel.

There is no sign of my Mr Meany. Then I all but stand on a heap of bones, an unkempt hump of a man passed out in a corner. I look again: it's him, my husband! I kick him awake and he stumbles, confused. Chris the dealer arrives from upstairs, grumpy at having been woken up ... He gives Boy 2 a rock and bag of brown and lectures him that there will be no more credit until this debt is settled ... Boy 2 stumbles into the early-morning, Black Label-littered ghetto street. I follow him down the steps, holding Joy. I want to kill him.

Next thing I see him at the corner garage on Soper Road. He's unwrapped the rock and is organising a hit for himself on top of the petrol pump. A cop car snails slowly past ... Oh, God, too much crack has made my heart go triple-speed – it seems to be thrusting out of my chest. I can't take it – what's wrong with him! He's gone insane! 'What's wrong with *you*?' asks another voice deep inside, but I thwack it down and continue cursing my ill-chosen, lunatic partner.

Finally, unable to get his attention, I flag a taxi down. We have no money for the cab ... We have a car with no fuel at the bottom of the hill, we have a baby, we have no money and we have no food ... All the way home Boy 2 smokes all the drugs he's managed to coerce from the Nigerian. He ignores me. He keeps it all to himself. God, how I hate him ...

In Westdene I stagger into the house, leaving him to deal with the taxi-man ... He walks in, chooses his R2 000 suede jacket from the wardrobe and leaves. I hear the taxi-man drive off, obviously happy with his deal ...

Oh, Jesus, this whole scene is starting to really choke me, things are going downhill fast. It seems like nothing can get worse. But if I think this is the nadir, I've got another thought coming ... Hell is sometimes a very long journey, and there are many miles still to cover.

CHAPTER 10

BUST

'Open the door …! Open the fucking door!!!'

Dush BANGbang DUSHbang!! I am cruelly ripped out of my smack gouge slumber, as Boy 2 thunders against the car window which is parked off Jorissen Street, near a big national bank early one Friday morning …

Joy is strapped in the baby chair at the back as usual and is observing his parents in an amused gurgle, tapping his bottle nonchalantly against the side of his chair.

I manage to pull up the lock just in time for Boy 2 to leap into the driver's seat, thrust the keys into the ignition, start the car and screech-squeal off into the early-morning bleary traffic. Just as the car lurches forward, a security guard comes into view, waving wildly. He's overweight, out of breath and by the time he arrives at our parking space, we're lost in the traffic.

'What the fuck – ?' I ask gunk-eyed. We've smoked ourselves senseless throughout the previous night and I am way beyond exhausted.

'Motherfuckers!' Boy 2 is pale, he's shaking as he steers the car through the bumper-to-bumper sea of early-morning 'let's-get-to-work-on-time' Jo'burg drivers.

'So did you get it?' I ask in a small, timid voice. I can see Mr Meany is in no mood for idle chat.

'Get it?' he shoots me an 'I-will-cut-you-into-little-pieces' look.

'No-o-ooo!!!!' he bellows. 'Of *course* I did not "get it"! I got bust!!! What the fuck do you think I was doing running down the road bashing on the window? Do you think I was doing that because I walked into the bank, cashed the cheque and then decided to pretend I was in *Dog Day Afternoon*?!'

Oh, boy. No cash, no drugs – is all I can think of. I am less concerned by whether my husband is OK, hurt, shot, photographed for *Crime Stop* or about to go to jail than the fact that we now have no means to get more shit.

'So ... ummm ... what happened?' I venture a pseudo-concerned 'I-am-your-wife-I-shall-stand-by-my-man' look on my face, not really sure if I can pull that one off!

It seems Boy 2 walked into the bank just as it opened. I had already nodded off in the parked car. The cheque that he was holding looked rather dodgy, I must admit. Although I had done the perfect three signatures the night before, in preparation for the big haul we were going to buy in the morning, on the way out the house Boy 2 had screamed at me for not doing something or other – the details are sketchy, as I try to recall them today.

But driving into Braamfontein, his edgy, accusative and scolding voice had caused me to cry. And three big, salty tears plopped onto the blue ink writing of the cheque that I was holding on my lap. I immediately tried to wipe off the saline show of emotions, but to no avail. My wipe caused a big smudge.

'Oh my fuck!' shouted Boy 2. He grabbed the cheque and furiously began to blot the wet patch … now it was really looking highly suspect.

'See what you've done!' he shrieked.

Oh, God! We had no more cheques and this was our only hope of getting stuff to appease the fast-approaching withdrawal that was already causing my nose to run and my brow to sweat and Boy 2 to behave like a maniac.

'I'm sure it will be OK, just say … just say …'

'Just say what?'

Now I was really starting to feel a tad nervous beside him. I could see where this was heading and I did not like the direction at all …

'Just say, your silly stupid bitch wife by mistake cried on the cheque 'cos she heard … um … her mother had died.'

There! Now, *that* was a good idea! Make the bank take pity on the cheque so they don't query it – give the cheque a history, an emotional background so that they feel embarrassed, give it the necessary stamp and signature and hand over the R900. I was so much a better criminal than this sorry excuse for my accomplice.

Boy 2 shoots an 'I-think-you-should-just-shut-the-fuck-up' glare my way and I close my eyes and fall into a slumber.

So, I later realise, after I'd gone into the land of smack, Boy 2 parked the car, locked it, waved farewell to his son like a crusader about to embark on some noble cruise, and walked into the bank. At the counter he handed in the cheque. He watched the teller look at the cheque and then start inspecting it more carefully. He began to get edgy. She then shot a look at Boy 2, picked up the cheque, walked to the back and, in low tones, began to discuss the matter with her manager.

Boy 2 was really edgy by now. The teller straightened her skirt, nodded and walked back towards the unkempt, wild-eyed man in dirty clothes waiting at the counter. She cleared her throat.

'Um … we need some type of ID in order to cash this cheque, and would you mind coming to the back with me? We just need to ask you a few things.'

At this point Boy 2 knew that it was over, something had happened and now the net was closing in. As he looked to the right, he saw his face on the bank television monitor and decide to take a run.

'I just need to get something,' he said, waving the teller away and darting for the glass door. Mercifully, the light went green, allowing him one-person access, just in time before the security guard, who had now been alerted to stop him from leaving the bank, closed in behind him.

Boy 2 was through, the lights went red. The security man was trapped in the bank on the other side …

That's where Boy 2 made the run and began bashing me out of my coma sleep to 'open the fucking door'.

Now Boy 2 was squealing though the traffic, missioning into the 'Brow, without cash. The area around his mouth was white and I could see the fury beating through the pores of his clammy skin. Realising I was in a danger zone, at the mercy of his wrath, I managed to keep quiet, biting my fist and feeling my heart pound against my rib cage.

In Soper Road our connection was waiting … loyal dealer, like a well-used street sign, as always in the assigned place. Boy 2 sauntered towards him. I watched Boy 2 gesticulating furiously, giving him the whole damn story. I kept close track of the dealer's every facial expression, this man who held all the keys to our pleasure – our drugs wrapped in plastic, stowed in his left cheek, like a little hamster. He seemed upset, wanting to have none of it, shaking his head.

I've become an ace lip-reader. Will he? Won't he? Will he? I make bets on the possibility that he will give us one of each and keep the other four rocks and four brown back … he slowly turns away and spits something out.

Yess-s-s!!! At least it's something!!! Oh, God, I need this hit so badly – I need to zoom and get fucked. Right now I need nothing more in this entire universe than to get away from it all and get high …

Within days of the botched bank job, events conspire and we get railroaded by family intervention. Someone in the company that we have defrauded calls my sister and Boy 2's sister and says, although they don't have sure-fire evidence, they highly suspect that the photo captured of the suspect in the bank is that of Boy 2. Their evidence, however, is blurred. His family panics, rallies together and literally gets us out of Jozi overnight.

This is what you call Lebanese organisation: they really do have a sense of brotherhood, understand the concept that unity is strength. At the very least, the Lebs realise that if your son has become a bank robber, you should get him out of town! And if he's got a good-for-nothing wife, you might as well drag her along too.

Our home in Westdene is packed up, rented out and we're delivered to the scintillating desert mining town in the North West called Klerksdorp. It's about 30 kilometres away from Ventersdorp, an AWB favourite and the conservative nature of the new setting is enough for anyone to want to get out of it and use as many drugs as the human constitution will allow.

On arrival, there's no chance to scout the town to score. Instead we are signed, sealed and delivered to a private clinic. For the next five days we are hooked up to drips of anaesthetic and put into sleep therapy: an answer to the family's mass-directed prayers.

Boy 2's mother has recently read about this method as a miracle cure for heroin addiction. She is a lioness, a true Mediterranean matriarch, and she conducts the operation with fierce capability and takes over with aplomb.

While we lie in anaesthetised Lala land, our baby is embraced, like a foundling, soon kitted out in the best clothing and waited on, hand on foot, by doting and loving aunts, granny and maids.

For five days we lie, like sleeping beasties on the morgue slab. Everyone is expecting us to wake up new people and start life again afresh, recovered and renewed. Alas … it's not to be.

———————

I wake up with a splitting headache to find I can't move my fingers properly. I discover this when trying to hold a cup of tea. My fingers are stiff, almost curled and as hard as I try to direct them, they don't seem to be doing what I want them to … I feel as if my life force has been sucked clean out of me, as though I have lain on a table with 300 vampires feasting at every vein and artery in my drug-ravaged body.

We move like zombies from day to day.

My mother-in-law has organised a newly-built townhouse for us on the outskirts of the town. I watch from my invalid perch as she carries in bags and bags of goods, choosing curtains, hanging them, putting carpets down, cutlery, crockery: everything she thinks we need, she has thought of. I should be grateful. I should be jumping up and down and clapping my hands in glee and saying: 'Thank you! Thank you!'

Instead, I sit – or, rather, droop – on the sofa, listless Lizzie, and scowl and sulk … Why hasn't she asked me if I like those ghastly green and orange curtains? I am the wife! Why is my opinion not important? (Whenever I am particularly sulky and self-pitying, I miraculously become 'the wife' – at all other times I usually behave in a completely unwifely and unmotherly way. I hardly cook – I have a full-time maid doing everything.)

Two months after emerging from sleep therapy, one morning we woke up and looked at each other. It was that old, dangerous look. It whispered: 'How about it?' Everything about that look screamed: 'Let's go and score!!!'

It was the first time I'd felt sexy, been excited, in ages. As though propelled by a deeper and more powerful force, we moved like automated machines to the car. Boy 2 had been given cash to pay the phone bill – at last there was a means to an end! Without a word I made bottles, packed two containers of baby food and we strapped our Joy in his seat. 'If my mother comes, tell her we've gone out with the baby on a picnic,' lied Boy 2 to the maid, Helena.

He filled the car with petrol and from the public phone at the fuel station, he phoned the dealer. We still knew his number. Although we had torn up our phone book to escape the temptation, that number was etched in my mind before I slept and when I woke up each morning, it was there. I knew it better than my own ID.

Today seemed like the happiest day of our lives. We were going home at last and we were going to score! 'This is like our honeymoon,' I enthused to my husband. 'Thank you! Thank you!'

'We're not going to get smack,' Boy 2 announced. He did not look at me. Catholic guilt. I nodded. I didn't care. Right now I longed for cocaine. Crack.

We both seemed to think that all our problems stemmed from the brown. If we didn't do heroin, everything would be fine. What we didn't realise then, of course – and would not realise for a number of years – was that we were addicts and it didn't matter what we touched, we suffered from the disease of *addiction*: the disease of more, of never enough, the disease of malcontent ...

Right now, watching him change into fifth gear and leaving the one-horse town behind, in the desert dust, for the first time in ages I felt a rush of love for Boy 2. Oh, God, I had longed for the open road – for that adrenaline rush, that stomach-churning feeling that we were about to go out and get high; 168 kilometres ahead of pure anticipatory pleasure.

I really felt like Mallory in *Natural Born Killers*. Yi-ha-a-aa!!

Seeing the beloved skyline of Ponte and the tower and all those downtown delicious grey buildings of Jo'burg appear like a magic castle in the sky, I felt as if I had been locked up in exile for years and this was my homecoming.

And feeling the imminent encroachment of ghetto-land Hillbrow with its hodge-podge of Africa, the colours, the different smells and textures filling the grey urban landscape, made my palms sweat, my skin tingle.

And when we saw our faithful dealer standing like a signpost in his usual place, we greeted and embraced him like the prodigal son. Oh, God, once we were all lost, but now we're all found ...

We found a nearby park and Boy 2 loaded the crack. I watched it sizzle and pop. The smell of cocaine, mixed with bicarb, had never smelt so good. Then it was my turn.

After such a long break, the hit is mind-blowing. I zoom off my head, my heart lurches, time stands still; everything comes to an amazing conclusion and climax, my eyes dilate into black hungry pools. Oh, my God!!!! I am home.

More. I want another. That's the very next thought. I watch Boy 2 – he's loading his second. My fingers want to grab that glass pipe and suck it. I know I must be patient, I watch him inhale. I watch him smoke. I am itching now ... he takes forever to look at me and breaks off a tiny piece. 'Uh ... don't you think that's a bit small ... ?' He shoots me that killer look. I bite my lip. Nail in the flesh. Crucified.

Oh, no, here we go again ...

An hour later I'm on my hands and knees between the glove compartment and the seat, searching for a crumb of crack.

'Get off the fucking floor – there's nothing there!' barks Boy 2, his eyes wild and pitch black. We're wired to the teeth ...

'I'm sure I dropped something,' I mutter.

'Get off the fucking floor – you're spinning me out.'

I sit on the seat, staring at the swings in the park. My heart is beating, I feel like I am freaking. The post-rock feel has a particular odour of death, it is a deep pit of nothingness, a screaming of GIVE ME MORRRRE! We need something to come down.

It's as though Boy 2 thinks the exact same thought at the exact same time. He starts the car. I dare not ask him what we're doing, but I am really hoping he might be planning what I'm thinking. At the corner café on Rockey Street he gets out. Three minutes later he's back and holding a roll of aluminium foil. We don't look at each other. Oh, my God, my entire being screams – 'Yes!!'

We are going to get some smack, oh yes – get rid of this spun-out feeling. Smoke some lovely gooey brown, feel that smoke encase me, feel that warm umbilical 'I'm a baby in the womb' feeling … heroin! Yes-s-s!!!

Oh, yes, here we go again … Smacked!

CHAPTER 11

PUTTING ON KILOMETRES

'Just give me that fucking book! Give it to me. I can't take this anymore.'

I sit in a crestfallen heap as Boy 2 towers above me, his hands outstretched, waiting for me to hand it over. I have *You and Your Baby,* a medical handbook, on my lap. I am, as usual, on page 165. It is a well-thumbed page, it is the page I always go to: *Diseases: Is Your Baby Ill?* It has a list of the many different diseases and symptoms a baby may suffer from. Over the last few months I have become obsessed with the book. Each day I wake up and look at Joy, who is nine months old now. I feel his little head, inspect his nappy – see the colour and constituency of his poo and rush to the book. I read each symptom carefully. I have become an ace diagnostic.

When I have put a complicated diagnosis together, I usually go to Boy 2 and say: 'I think our child has malaria', or 'I think Joy has yellow fever/bilharzia/rubella'.

At first Boy 2 buys into my neurosis and reads the book as carefully as I do, feels Joy's temperature, stares at his stools that I have religiously collected and looks bewildered. However, lately he has begun to suspect that his wife is losing the plot. Somewhat!

'This is all bullshit!' he fumes, then grabs the book and – with one fell swoop – rips at the middle section, all the pages I love. I watch as he tears my obsession apart. It feels like he is ripping my heart, my soul in two.

'I think I want to take his poo to a laboratory to get it tested,' I manage to whisper.

I'm not sure when it happened, or even why, really, although I have a few theories, but over time I became obsessed that my child was sick. While everyone cooed around him and he gurgled and smiled, I knew deep in my pit that all was not well. How could it be? I had imbibed drugs through a lot of my pregnancy and I could not believe he could possibly be alright after all he'd been through. I felt hopeless and guilty. I knew I was a complete failure as a mother and the only thing I could latch onto was this handbook.

From the outset, the mother thing had befuddled me: I never really knew why the baby cried. Boy 2 would usually jump up before me anyway and cradle and comfort him. I would watch perplexed, almost envious at the bond Boy 2 shared with our son. I felt more and more useless as time passed. I was also not able to forget the mutilation I had endured during his birth … the scar from the episiotomy stitch still felt lumpy and sensitive … and I was bored – I was so fucking bored. Days in the one-horse desert town dragged on and on. I seemed to spend more and more time lounging on the sofa watching re-runs of *The Bold and the Beautiful*. I knew every eyelash on Brooke's face, every quiver of Taylor's lip. I knew their outfits, their motives, the intimate details of their lives. I knew these Forresters better than I knew myself. I was a sponge, a soap opera vampire. It felt as if my life had become a joke.

Finally, Boy 2 began to lose patience with me. Who was this woman who occupied space around the house? I did not cook, I did not clean. I was so depressed that I could hardly move when the baby cried. To dress him was an insurmountable task most times. Combing my hair was like climbing Everest. My hands were still not doing things in the same way as before the sleep therapy. With the great escape to the North West, a black deep pit of depression had moved in.

I could not stand the sweltering heat of the town. The sweat, the stench, the ugly people who reminded me of a *Jerry Springer Show* white-trash interbred audience … And the black people cowering and moving around as donkey servants. They walked burdened and padded with instructions from white *base* who had not taken one step forward into the new South Africa. It was 1997. It may as well have been 1947.

I stood outside the circle of everything. Boy 2's family was close-knit and often congregated. I would find myself at lunches and dinners … sitting far away, smoking my 30th cigarette of the day … watching and wishing to be somewhere else. Finally, I would find myself in a circle of the Lebanese men who at least smiled and tried to joke with me while the women stood watching from the kitchen windows chopping vegetables, making *kibbie, taboulleh,* mixing sauces, cooking, cooking, chopping and hissing in hushed tones at the bad, bad daughter-in-law, the bad wife poor Boy 2 had been dumped with. I knew they spoke ill of me. It made me want to be much worse, do less, fail more. I did not have to the energy or inclination to do anything about their perceptions and judgements, because basically they were all spot-on. I *was* dreadful. I *was a* bad wife, bad mother, bad junkie, bad human being – and I couldn't or wouldn't do a fucking thing about it.

'What shall we do today?' Boy 2 would say every morning, hoping one day I would come up with something innovative and exciting.

'Let's go to Jo'burg … ' was all I'd say, and he'd shoot a murderous look at me. I'd listen really carefully to his every move, hoping, wishing, praying to hear 'getting-ready-to-go-to-Jo'burg' moves. And then if I heard the kitchen drawer bang open and closed – I knew he'd be getting the foil.

Boy 2 had begun to terrify me. As my power over my existence seeped away, like Sunday leftovers down a gargling drain, he began to take on an ogre-like presence. Perhaps it was a combination of cocaine, paranoia, small-town cabin fever – perhaps it had everything to do with the fact that he had crossed physically violent boundaries with me. Once someone hits you, you never quite walk as closely or feel as safe with that person again.

So I placed all my longings for love on that aluminium silver paper.

The foil meant everything. The foil meant we were going. Going meant everything. Going meant escaping the tedium of jobless, useless days, escaping the sense of failure that embalmed me as I sat on that gaudy couch, watching the baby crawl and the maid change him when he was wet. In the end scoring was my only passion, all I ever really wanted to do ...

_____

We put 148 000 kilometres on the car in one year, driving to and from Jo'burg once a day, seven days a week, 168 kilometres there and 168 kilometres back ...

Boy 2 became an expert ETA (expected time of arrival) man. He could estimate within the minute what time we would arrive at the hotel in Hillbrow to meet the dealer. Within minutes of the agreed time, we would swoop in from the highway, down below the concrete bridge under Harrow Road, up past the Hillbrow park and *voila*! We'd be there and the dealer would be there and it would somehow feel like magic, as if by the hand of God we had all found each other.

'It's a pity you can't get a job doing this,' I said to him once. 'You're really good at it, you know, estimating the whole time thing.'

It was the nicest thing I'd said to him in months.

'Yeah, well, I don't think I've seen any jobs like that advertised lately: "Junkie needed who arrives on time to score. Apply within."' He snarled.

Everyone kept telling *me* to get a job. His aunt would hint at it and then his mother would come straight out with it. 'Why don't you go and ask at the local supermarket for some work?' she'd say at least once a week as she reversed her massive BMW out of our driveway, looking through her Ralph Lauren sunglasses and her newly-set hair glistening red in the beating sun.

I could not even look at her, she made me so angry. I! Work as a check-out girl, pack packets at the till ... I!? I, who had been to university, who had a degree, I who had an Einstein-like IQ, I, who was once Miss Somebody – I? Never!

What made my feelings of uselessness and boredom even worse was when I occasionally stumbled upon an article in the Johannesburg newspaper *The Star* about a friend, or someone I had known in my other life, who was doing really well: performing in a play, directing a movie, winning an award for a music video. Living a life. It would depress me deeply and I would read the snippet over and over again and feel that the possibility of me ever returning to a real, productive and creative life, was growing smaller and smaller by the day. I was becoming invisible.

Each time we went into Jo'burg, we never really *went* there. We drove in, picked up the stuff, smoked some and then immediately missioned out. We were paranoid about Boy 2's family noticing we were missing, so we rushed back to make sure we weren't away for more than three or four hours. It never even felt like we were there. We just floated on the edges, in and out, in and out. Life in the big city carried on – ignored and disregarded us. We were no longer anything or anyone. We'd even stopped being gossip subject fodder at industry dinner parties … no-one cared. We might as well have been dead. In truth, we *were* dead.

CHAPTER 12

PUTTING ON KILOGRAMS

'Kill yourself,' the voice said. *'Kill yourself.'*

I was pregnant! Again! Oh, God. No!!!

If seeing those two blue stripes appear on that home pregnancy test the first time round in early 1996 had made me weep, the second time round sent me into a depression as dark and deep as some forlorn, pillaged oil-well in Iraq.

I am comatose by the news. I am not even handling mothering one child, neither of us is. We are not working. We are driving almost daily to Jo'burg to score. Now we are expecting another. This is insane. I do not have any money of my own, not even a bank card or an ID book. I cannot afford to buy my own cigarettes. I have to beg Boy 2, who has to keep getting handouts from his family. The line of begging bowl hands is growing and now there is this new life multiplying inside me … I can't comprehend it … it's all too much …

'We can't do this,' I say in a hoarse whisper, staring at the incriminating test. 'How are we going to? We can't

– you know – do this,' I say again. It seems like I am talking Swahili. He stares ahead, blank wall.

His fists are clenched, knuckles white.

'Well, we can't *not* do it either,' he says.

Oh, you silly Catholic!

'But how?' I say.

He is silent for a very long time.

'Don't worry – we will,' says he.

———————

'Hi, honey, I'm home!'

He walks in, his grey suit and tie perfect.

'Hi, darling, how was your day?'

She pecks him on the cheek, wipes her hands on her spotless apron. The smell of roast beef and apple pie wafts through the kitchen. Baby crawls in and gurgles when he sees Daddy. 'What a neat little family we have!' she thinks, and smiles.

She fixes him a martini. He sits in his favourite armchair. He opens the newspaper she has thoughtfully left beside it. He reads. Soothing music tinkles in the background. 'Gee, honey, your hair looks nice in that style!' he remarks.

The dream never goes away. It's always in the back of my head as I survey the loop of my life, the calamity of my days. Not a single 'Hi, honey, I'm home' in this wasteland world.

———————

I don't know how-I don't know how-I don't know how ... I keep thinking this thought over and over again. Then the voice that has been waiting to pounce for many moons at last rears its ugly serpentine head.

'Kill yourself.'

It says this very casually, very softly, but oh so succinctly, with such authority. *'Kill yourself.'*

And so begins my journey into carrying a new life and thinking of ways and means to end my own.

The baby has been conceived at the ironing board. We have been attempting yet another withdrawal session. Withdrawing these days is usually suggested by Boy 2. I just go along with whatever he says. He's the boss now – I'm too down and dark to think of anything myself anymore.

It seems that the male, when withdrawing from drugs, immediately starts regaining sensation in his dick. Boy 2 always got horny about 24 hours after the last hit.

Six weeks earlier, I'm standing in the spare room leaning on the ironing board when I feel him behind me. I let him have his way and, once again, all it takes is a three-minute session to create a whole new life.

'What would you like to do today?' says Boy 2.

'Die. Kill myself.' My mind screams. I try to look upbeat.

'Ummm not sure …' I say. 'You know … we could … you know … I don't know, really – what do *you* want to do?' Throw it in his court.

Of course we go. To Jo'burg. Don't even have to say it anymore. We can't stop. The addiction grows; the need expands and gobbles everything in sight ... Oh, my God, our reality has become a butt end of pointlessness and oblivion.

My stomach grows quickly this time, even though I am not eating a lot. This pregnancy is so unlike the first one. At least then I was naïve and did not know what I was in for. This time round I feel dark and heavy. Immediately. I am like an animal moving from resting place to resting place, seeking shade, seeking quiet, seeking an end. I lug my body, dragging it like a tatty blow-up blanket around with me. The other – the motherless self – watches, horrified at the changing body.

And the annihilation field of my mind grows and grows. Each day I wake up and the voice says: *'Kill yourself.'*

It gets louder. It's incredible how that voice swallows up spaces, it colonises everything, like some crazy ebola virus.

And now I start thinking of ways and means to do it.

———————————

I cannot shoot myself. I don't have a gun. Boy 2's brother has one ... but I don't think I will be able to get my hands on it.

I think of drowning myself in the local dam. We go there one morning to break the monotony. Boy 2 is trying really hard to think of things to do that don't entail driving to score. We sit at the edge of the lapping water and I imagine walking forward, walking into the silvery moving surface and going under, under, until I am no more ... locked in the tangled embrace of seaweed.

Like Ingrid Jonker, but at least she left something behind – great, working poems ... I have contributed nothing. No-one will remember me for anything. Except perhaps unfulfilled potential. The thought of no-one at my funeral depresses me deeply. Anyway, drowning is impractical: I am a good swimmer and in all probability, my body – especially with a growing tummy – will refuse to stay under, like a stubborn cork.

Later that evening, I come across insecticide and tick medicine for the dog, in the top kitchen cupboard. It's clearly labelled 'Poison'. I read the ingredients and warnings carefully. But I am terrified that if I take it, it will not be completely effective and kill me, but rather leave me maimed or brain-damaged. Worse still, it could kill or retard the unborn child. *'You're thinking far too logically for a suicide,'* the voice scolds. *'Pull yourself together. Kill yourself.'*

A month later I find myself at 6 am in the laundry at the back of the house. I am all alone besides the baby who is growing fast in my belly. I have a tie in my hand. I am breathing quickly. I put it round my neck and begin to pull tighter. 'That's it! I will strangle myself ...'

But it's absurd, really, for as it gets tighter and tighter, my hand releases it involuntarily ... *'You can't strangle yourself, stupid, you've got to hang yourself, from the tree outside.'* The voice laughs at me. Hang myself ...? Oh, no, that just feels too Absalom-ish, too Biblical.

With each failed idea, I feel more and more imprisoned in this body of mine ... it feels like I am living trapped alive, like some animal, caught in the metal jaws of a snare. There is no escape. I can't even find a way to kill myself.

Finally all that is left is the age-old, very popular and rather boring method of cutting the wrist and bleeding to death ... But this one is far more complicated than it first appears. Firstly, it's going to require a whole few hours where I am alone, where there is no-one to disturb me after I've slit the wrist and I lie in a warm bath and slowly feel the life force eke out of me ...

But, still, this plan seems to be the closest one to a practically sound one that I've come up with so far.

I begin planning to get Boy 2 out the house, Joy to his grandmother and the maid not to come to work ... It takes weeks and finally the day dawns. It's a Wednesday. I have given the maid the morning off. Boy 2 is off to see *Titanic* at the local cinema, 9.30 am show and he's organised Joy to be baby-sat by his grandmother. I decline the invitation to the movie and say I want some time on my own ... oh, boy, and how!

I have decided to do the job with a litre Coke bottle. I have checked all the knives in the house and none of them are sharp enough. I wave Boy and Joy goodbye. My heart aches a dull sorrow and the early-morning light blinds me temporarily. *'This is the last time you will see your family.*

Wave goodbye ...' the voice whispers. A lone tear squeezes out the side of my lid ... it's tiny.

Like a robot, I retrieve the bottle I have hidden in the garage. I sit near the flower bed. I take the bottle and smash it against a large stone. It shatters and jaggers. I hold a perfectly sharp, ugly-edged weapon in my hand.

I slowly look at my white unmarked wrist. It looks so sad – so nothing in this early blank light. I have waited long for this moment and yet I don't feel a thing. Without a second thought, I come down with my right hand – slice one hard, deep and decisive shot. I have not thought which direction to cut in and in that moment the glass moves across horizontal. I later discover it's impossible to die like this – you have to go the vertical route.

The slice is deep. I can see the ravine – the skin parted like the Red Sea pictures from Sunday school classes when I was five. I watch the blood begin to flow. I have filled a bath ready to hold me in death – I don't bother to go there. I know deep down that I have botched this. I begin to weep – the aloneness of it all terrifies. Boy 2 has his mother's cellphone. I call him from the neighbour's house. I tell her I have had an accident and I need to call my husband. He is on his way to the movie house.

'I've done something,' I say. 'Can you come back here? Please.'

He's back at the house in minutes. He sees my wrist. He looks angry.

'I need to get something to close it,' is all I can say. 'Not the doctor, it's not that deep, I don't think. The chemist – can we get something on your mother's account?'

Of course we can't pay – we never have any cash, ever, it all goes on smoke.

That's how we live. On other people's money. There's a food account, a chemist account, a video account. Boy 2 just signs and his family pays. He hates it; I don't seem to give a fuck. The dreadful daughter-in-law, I have got used to that name.

And when we need cash I steal it. From his mother's bag. She always seems to have wads, I never think she'll notice. Boy 2 is clever – he never gets his hands dirty. It's always me, the thief. When I hand it over he looks disapproving, but the next thing the car is reversing and we're off to Jo'burg.

Lately he's been teaching his nephew English at his older brother's double-storey house. Not much teaching gets done. Boy 2 listens to music and works on his film script. Nephew plays Playstation. I come along with Joy, 'cos I have nothing better to do.

And somehow I usually land up with my fingers in his brother's wife's handbag – the temptation of stealing a few R100 notes is too good to miss.

The maid sees me one morning and reports me to the madam. All hell breaks loose. Boy 2's brother confronts him about his thieving, good-for-nothing wife. A fight ensues. Boy 2's brother takes the cricket bat and, in true Leb gang style, breaks his brother's leg. We don't go back to the house.

So now Boy 2 is on crutches, hobbling like some robot tramp and right now I have a wrist that is streaming with my red life force.

The chemist gives me a yellow ointment to close wounds. It does not need stitches. I tell him I cut the wrist while washing the dishes. A wine glass broke in the water. He doesn't look like he gives a damn, never mind believes me.

I go to *Titanic* with Boy 2. My wrist beats and aches throughout the scenes where Leonardo and Kate fall in love on the ill-fated ship.

I wear long-sleeved shirts for the rest of summer, afraid that Boy 2's mother or sister will find out I'm a basket case. *'What a failure!'* the voice mocks. *'You can't even kill yourself!'*

I surrender. I decide to wait, give birth and then – as soon as the baby is born and someone has taken it away from me to get cleaned – I will jump off the hospital roof.

CHAPTER 13

TOO LOW TO JUMP

The hospital is only two floors high. If I jump from the roof I shall break my legs and/or my arms, at the very worst. Once again my death plans are foiled. I look down at my three-hour-old son suckling like a mewling kitten at my heavy breasts. There is something so sweet, so defenceless about this little thing. *'Ah, life is bigger … bigger than you …'* I hear Michael Stipe singing in the back of my mind. And right now I know nothing but that to die is not that easy, and to live is not easy either. Right now I inhabit a space between the two.

Baby 2, whom we call Day, is born quickly and much more painlessly in the private hospital with my own ward and good attentive doctors. This time round, it's much easier than the birth of my first. I have also not been taking as many drugs as the first time – being further away from the source in some ways has helped …

But the depression has not lifted – it just gets more and more intense. Where some people may suffer from a touch of post-partum depression, I have suffered from it right through the pregnancy and now it seems to have moved in for good, set to stay. Joy is not yet 19 months, he's still drinking bottles, not able to dress himself, wearing nappies ... Day needs 24/7 attention, like all new-born babies do ... Oh, God, and I need a free pass to a mental asylum.

I do not know how I get through days. They drag from morning into the night into morning, looping the same old same old. Boy 2 and I no longer sleep in the same room. He sleeps with Joy in one and I sleep with Day in the other. I breast-feed the baby until, withdrawing yet again from smack, I tug him off in exasperation one morning and bring out the bottles ...

I am this empty cow – nothing inside – trying to appease these two needy, hungry sons who want and want and want ... I start thinking that perhaps even though I have not killed myself, I should think of ways to kill the entire family ... what else are we going to do? There is nothing inside that tells me anything is going to be OK.

Boy 2 hardly talks to me anymore. All his dreams of becoming a famous director like Fellini dash as each day passes. The disappointment he feels for his life manifests with certain permanence ... And his anger grows.

My depression is both chemical and hormonal. I move from making one meal to making another meal. It never seems to stop – the feeding requirements, the hungry mouths that open and close, open and close like greedy guppies and because I have tits and am called 'woman', I am expected to miraculously prepare these meals.

Boy 2's mother is an expert cook and nothing I make comes close to what she prepares. I cannot cook and I cannot kill myself.

I spend the time between making meals huddled on the couch. Dragging myself through long, relentless days, wearing tracksuits, not washing my hair, watching the oil gather ... I hate bathing, feeling water on my skin.

'What are you doing here?' Boy 2 glares at me one evening. 'We don't need you, you know. You're just taking up space ... why don't you sleep outside, sleep in the fucking car?'

He has both babies in his arms. Day is drinking his bottle ... and Joy is watching me from his dad's lap. They are a wall of male gaze. They despise me. I can feel it. I know they don't need me. But what to do, what to do with this self?

———————

It's 2 am. I find myself with a broken Coke bottle in the dark; I hold it inches from the unsuspecting neck of my husband. His jugular throbs in the moonlight. I sit like this for hours. I am close to killing him. If I kill him, then I will have to kill my two sons and then myself. *'Well, you haven't got it together to do **yourself** in, so what makes you think you are now going to be able to do four people?'* the voice sneers.

By morning light I know that if I don't get drugs today, something terrible will happen ... I literally go on bended knees, begging Boy 2 to take me to Jo'burg.

'If you don't get me stuff, if you don't take me there, I am going to kill the babies. I can't cope today, please, please, please!'

'We have no money. Organise and we can go,' he says.

Lately we've been sinking to the all-time low of pawning nappies. I have worked out a neat, effective, albeit pathetic, system. I buy two packets of disposables at the supermarket where my mother-in-law has an account. Boy 2 signs, then I take the nappies to a larger supermarket down the road and walk in and say:

'I wonder if you can help me? My mother bought too many nappies, not knowing that I have already bought some. Could I please get a refund?'

No-one seems to mind, the refund's processed and one two three I'm out of there – with R300 in hand.

Last month we borrowed his brother's lawnmower before he kneecapped Boy 2 and we pawned it and got another R300 for it. We never got round to cutting the grass. When we junkies need the stuff, we always find ways and means to get it. Always. We are masters of invention. I smile to myself as I get in the car, show the cash. We head off for the big concrete city to appease the shakes and get high.

CHAPTER 14

RIPPED

'I would like to take your children away ... for the day. Give you a break; you need it, I'm sure. Would you pack some clothes, please?' My mother-in-law addresses me coldly. She looks at my filthy tracksuit and unwashed hair ... I can see her disdain, her contempt. She is a picture of elegance, the queen of the town, turned out at every level ... she never has a hair out of place. I look like *dreck*, an unkempt, horrid specimen.

I'm relieved at the promise of a break; maybe we can get away and score. Dutifully I pack some clothes for the two boys, bottles and formula, and wave the troop goodbye. Boy 2 is silent, distracted. When I suggest a trip to Jo'burg, he wordlessly agrees and within minutes we're out on the highway off to Smack Crack Lala Land.

By late afternoon we're back and there's no sign of the boys. He makes a call out of my earshot. He tells me his mom will look after them for the night ... I don't think anything of it, I'm content, we still have another hit to smoke and here's a rare break from duty. A baby-free night lies ahead.

By 4 pm the following day there is still no sign of my children. I am starting to get worried. I have this dull, nervous feeling about it all. 'What do you think is going on?'

I ask him. He is distracted, can't look at me … And then it's as though a torrent, a wave hits. She's taken them! I know it deep down. They are not here and they are not coming back. Oh, God, they have taken my children!

'Motherfuckers!!!' I scream and I begin to run. I am running up the hill, seven kilometres away, towards her glass palace, towards the wicked mother-in-law who has taken my two young cubs. It takes me 15 minutes to run there. I thunder down the driveway, screech towards the front door. Panting like a mad dog, I throw myself against the door and knock and knock and ring the bell over and over. Boy 2 has followed me all the way, trying to get me into the car. He jumps out, leaving the door open.

There are a lot of luxury cars parked in the driveway. I don't notice. I am here to get my boys. My mother-in-law opens the door, she's made up like a queen, elegant evening wear, chunky jewellery adorns her ears and neck. The maid stands behind her holding Day. He sees me and breaks out in a gurgling smile, outstretched arms. I lurch towards him and am apprehended by the cruel kidnapper.

'Get out of this house, you drug addict whore! Get out! You will never see these children again!' She snarls at me, stepping right up close to my face. She's fearless.

'Fuck you! Fuck you! FUCK YOU!' I scream and lurch out for my son.

In the background the gentle tinkle of glasses, mood music, Mantovani, can be heard. They are entertaining tonight, a rotary function and my entrance coincides with the host making his welcome toast and opening speech.

I try to push her out the way, punch her, thrash her – I do what I have to – they have taken my flesh, I must retrieve it. As I punch her, in one fell swoop Boy 2 dashes to his mother's rescue, grips me and shoves me to the floor, me a screeching banshee as he pins me down and slaps me. I always knew it was his mother that he would run to. Sad Oedipus.

I kick and shriek, but he's got me down. He drags me out, a chaotic ball of hysteria, the big white door slams shut behind me, putting the nail, the wedge, between me and my babies. I'm thrown into the front seat, he starts the car and screeches off. Sonless, like a beast untamed, I howl and wail. It mingles with the brakes and gear changes as he hurtles the car this way and that.

He is shaken beyond his normal veneer of dead cut-off cool. He grabs my head and thrashes it into the steering wheel. 'Why? Why? Why did you do that?' over and over again. I feel my hairline break out into a pool of matty blood. 'Why? Why? Why?' He moans and yells.

Now he's opened the door on the passenger side, he's speeding at 140 km/h and he's holding me by the back of my head, my face inches from the rushing by of tar.

'Why? Why? Why did you have to fucking do that!?' Over and over again … All his hatred for me is exploding, it has no bounds. Oh, Jesus, I am going to die. Not by my own hand – he is going to kill me.

There is not an inch of exaggeration when I say this was by far the worst night of my life. Ever. I do not think there can ever be another night like this. The rape, the drugs, the withdrawal, the birth – all these incidents pale in comparison with this Kristallnacht, this Night of the Long Knives.

Back at the house I fall, trip in … I head for the kitchen. I pull out the bread knife … I run to the bathroom and start making slices, cuts, nicks … I see the blood. I want to stab that dagger into my solar plexus. Kill. Slice … The anger, the powerlessness, the hopelessness of it all … It needs big gestures … Greek amphitheatre ones. Nothing can meet the feelings running rampant inside … I cannot contain them … He bashes at the door. I will not open. He bashes through it. He takes the knife off me. He cuts himself … We are bleeding, like Sid and Nancy, Kurt and Courtney … We have nothing … so empty and so fucked … There is nothing left between us. I could kill him. He could kill me. It would all mean nothing … and then I know what to do …

'You do not do you do not do anymore black shoe …' chants the voice in my head.

I pull on my black trousers, black jersey, black jacket, black boots and I rub black on my face, my hands … I am all black … I will disappear. I run out, through the house. I am on the road … I am running in the black night. I am no-one. I have crossed over to the other side … *'This is the end beautiful friend the end …'* I hear it. The music surrounds and accompanies me … Now I know where I am running to … I am heading for that highway … It is where those great trucks go, up and down, up and down, back and forth … carrying goods from one part of this land to another, flying at outrageous speeds, they will not see me melted on the tar … I shall lie on that big black road and with no moon out tonight I shall be crushed, I shall disappear on that tar. It shall be my bed, my final resting place, still warm from the beating hot daytime sun. I am free. I am running. At last, oh God yes, at last I am free.

He gets to me before I reach it. He cuts me off. He fells me like a rabbit catcher. He pulls me back. He snares me. He bundles me back like a naughty errant parcel. I am weak. I cannot run. He beats me. In all ways.

He takes me home. 'Pack,' he says. He tells me to go. He says: 'Tomorrow I will go to rehab. You cannot stay here. The children will stay with my mother. I will take you tomorrow to Jo'burg. You will have to stay with a friend or your family. You can't stay here.'

This is the last night I ever spend with my husband.

CHAPTER 15

LOOK-BACK TIME

It has taken me months to write this chapter. I have blocked it and run away from it, excused myself, played truant with the page ... yet at last, on 13 April 2005, I cannot hide from it any longer. Strangely, I get to it on the day of my wedding anniversary, the day Boy 2 and I got married to each other nine years ago. We have been parted for almost six of them. I am on the coast tying up the book when I finally sit down to write about it ... and as it comes back, gargling and rushing back and forth like too much septic mouth wash, the worst night of my life, I am suddenly bang crashed by a dark realisation so deep it cuts me to the core:

Maybe, just maybe ... he knew all along that our babies would be taken from me! Perhaps he planned it with his mother and his family ... Oh God! Maybe he knew! He knew! ... My mind runs wild with this thought ... I can see it all now, he was complicit all along, the way he avoided me, those half-baked, non-committal answers. Like the waves out here, thundering in and out on the edge of the house I am writing in at the coast, everything comes crashing clear ... I do not know why I have never considered this scenario before and why today, it hurts me so.

Of course I know now, looking back, the babies being taken away was all for the best and today we are all alive and well because of that intervention. But something about that night – the manner in which it was done, my need to die and all that black, the nauseating shock – makes me break inside when I remember it. I crack a little more each time, like some rock split by a great unexpected underworld tremor. I miss my boys for the time I lost with them. The bedrock of my pain, it makes me feel so sad. So fucking sad. I think it always will.

PART 2

THE TWILIGHT ZONE

CHAPTER 16

HOME TIME

When all else fails, go home. But what if home doesn't want you?

Home is where the heart is, the old saying goes. But home was so remote. 'Home is just emotion sticking in my throat …' sang Lene Lovich. I remember her from 1980: *'Let's go to your place …'*

Well, the problem with going home was that no-one really wanted to have me there. Who could blame them? A junkie who could not be trusted, with her fingers in handbags, stealing, taking, pawning whatever she could lay her hands on, for her fix. Angry, irrational, blaming, crazy diatribes spring from my mouth … Anyone who gets in my way I lacerate with my poison tongue – they could go on forever, the adjectives of put-off.

Perhaps now, more than ever – because of the shock of the babies being taken and those days leading up to that awful event – I was at an all-time low crazy space … I did not have my senses about me in any way.

With Boy 2 finally throwing the towel in on our using, I was furious and felt deeply betrayed. Now I was left all alone – there was not one hair, not one cell on my body that wanted to stop using drugs. In fact, the events of late had just catapulted me into a ravenous, insatiable hunger for cocktails of chemical substance delirium.

The following day, we drove to Jo'burg, not a word was spoken. Boy 2 had his bags packed for rehab. I had got two suitcases of stuff together and my R30 000 video camera: I thought I might make a movie sometime! Without a word we picked up one rock and one bag of brown and smoked a final hit together in a park. All around, pathetic plastic wrappers fluttered in the wind. It felt like a full stop to a whole life.

Thereafter he dropped me at my eldest sister's spot in Troyeville ... Still silence. There was nothing left between us. The emptiness of overness is what it was. As he drove off, my first and only idea was to get a lift from someone to Bob's Bar, get drunk and maybe pick up someone, get them to score and maybe get lucky and get laid ... I had been faithful, if you can call it that. More accurately, I had been completely fidelity-bound to Boy 2 for over seven years and now, going along with my general nihilistic vibe, I just wanted to meet and fuck as many men as possible. To hurt him, get back at him, but really to hurt myself more than anything ... His going to rehab felt like the worst of betrayals, far more serious than him taking on 300 lovers ...

———————————

My sister stands before me. Stern unchanging robot. She is my big sister, the one who taught me all I know about rebellion and courage as a child. She is also my nemesis, the eagle shadow that up until this point has hung over and strangled me all of my life. Highly talented, a child ingénue, like a little Mozart she is tinkling piano concertos at an unusually young age. It blows it for the rest of us ... I can't catch up to her, ever. She is always 20 steps ahead, so I choose the black sheep role in the family instead. It's much easier, much less hassle, less responsibility and even though everyone makes fun of me and underestimates me, it's somehow safer here in this outside sheep pen of no effort.

'If you go out tonight, I promise you, you will find your bags packed out on the pavement in the morning,' she threatens, Nazi prison guard. 'You cannot come into my house and do what you like, there are rules here,' she snarls.

Without a word, I swing on my leather jacket and start to walk.

'You've just lost your children. Don't you care, aren't you ashamed of yourself!?' she screams after me.

Fuck her. Fuck everyone. I clutch the R100 crumpled note that I've managed to pilfer from her purse as she answers her phone. Fuck it all!!!

No babies no husband no fucking anything. I will make sure I make this new-found single status work for me. And I will smile as I do it. Whatever else I am, I know I am a survivor with an ability to make everything seem like it is exactly the way I want it to be.

———

At Bob's Bar I hook up with Rory, the Irish journalist who's an alcoholic crazy soul and a straight magnet for my madness. We snort handfuls of drugs and drink ourselves into a coma. At 3 am, giggling like two maniacs, we trip-fall out the car on the pavement outside my sister's home. As we push the wooden gate open leading towards her front door, he pulls out his beer-laden prick and pees in her pot plants, missing the spot and pissing all over her red stone veranda. We fall over in a heap of hilarity. I haven't had such a good time in years! She's comes out, huge billowy madam in her nightgown.

'What the hell do you think you're doing!?' she barks. We giggle, naughty children, helplessly.

'Good evening,' says Rory, saluting.

'Get inside!' she shouts at me. 'Get inside right now! Who the hell is this man!? He's not coming into my house.'

'You know ... he's Rory. He's won awards for the stuff he's written for *Business Today* or *Financial* whatssit, whatever. He's a very good writer. You know,' I drawl.

'Get inside now!' she yells.

'You're not my mother,' I slur. 'You can't tell me what to do ... ' She glowers at me, her face unmoving, a cold rock.

'Come,' I say to Rory. 'Let's go to your place. My sister's a bit hectic ... hey, isn't that line from a Lene Lovich song? *Let's go to your place ...*' I sing.

Giggling, we stagger back to his car and head for his spot in Kensington.

Next morning, true to her word, my bags are packed waiting to be picked up.

'All my bags are packed, I'm ready to go ...' I whistle as I leave. Damn Peter, Paul and whatsherface! I have been kicked out after 14 hours – not bad for someone who's homeless. This is the first of many evictions that occur over the next few months.

'I've been thrown out, can I come and stay at your place?' I bend down to speak to Rory, bleary with a hangover. He shrugs and opens the passenger door. I feel nothing. I am free, no children, no husband – at last I can do exactly what I please.

'You've just had your children taken from you ... aren't you ashamed of yourself!? Aren't you ...' screams my sister as our car pulls off. Fuck you. Fuck everyone.

'Do you have any dagga? Or should we get some crack?' I ask my new companion.

Within days we are screaming and fighting like two rabid dogs. We find ourselves in a bar late one night. It's like a scene from *Leaving Las Vegas* where we sit facing a mirror, shouting drunken, slurred insults at each other. He sees my face in the mirror and throws a shooter glass at my reflection. It's late out on dead downtown, we are two lost, tired and angry souls. It's the fear, the loathing – we are mirroring each other. Fuck it all.

Seven days later he throws me out, after yet another bad mad fight. Next stop: my brother's house. Seems like I'm running out of options.

———————

'You can't stay here anymore, you're going to have to go.' I've been at my brother's place for 10 days. I'm hardly there, I have been missioning to the 'Brow daily, pawning his wife's and his possessions, getting drugs and then going to Bob's Bar. Now his wife doesn't want me there. Wonder why! Silly cow.

I stare at him. So? What do I do now? All wide-eyed and manipulative. I've become a child.

'I'm going to pay for you to stay in a hotel close by,' he says. My sweet little brother – he's the last and only person on the planet who gives a fuck about me. Problem is I can't see it. I can't see anything anymore except for finding ways and means to get loaded.

'Cool,' I say. 'Where is it?'

———————

I'm kicked out of the plush hotel in Parktown for trying to steal the bolted-down television in my bedroom. My brother picks me up.

'I've had enough of you,' he says, the pain is in his eyes. I don't see it.

'Look at you! You're disgusting! Look at you with your fucking Doc Martens – what's wrong with you!? Aren't you trying to get your kids back?'

I'm eyeing his new Nokia that's peeping out of the back pocket of his Levis.

'You know, I wish I had a gun and then I could give it to you so you could shoot yourself. Look at you. I can't bear seeing you like this!' He stifles a sob.

I stare back at him. Nothing penetrates. Where am I going to get cash to score?

'Listen here,' he says finally, sighing deep tiredness. 'I am giving you one more chance. I have found a hotel at the end of town so you are as far away as possible from all of us. I am going to pay for you up front for a week, and then you must make a plan – get a job – I don't know what – but I am giving you a week to come up with something.'

I don't hear anything – I am thinking of that cellphone as we drive down Jules Street, it's right in the deep south. Maybe he'll give me some cash. I mean, how I am supposed to eat!? He carries my bag to my room on the fourth floor. The green carpets give the place a sickly vibe. The hotel feels like it's at the end of the world. Called The Statesman, it's a real hooker and gangsta joint. He pays at the reception and gives me R300.

'There. I can't give you more – you're getting breakfast and dinner here. Please don't use this money for drugs.'

I hardly see him walk away or wave goodbye. I am already working out a plan, missioning in my mind to the 'Brow, to go and score.

Ninety minutes later I am back in my room with the stash ... Three rocks, three brown. Oh yeah, it's party time!! The best thing about my current status is that I no longer have to wait for the titbits Boy 2 has been throwing at me for who knows how long ... No! All the stuff is mine! And my greed grows and grows – it's enormous, never ending. It exposes all the hungry spaces inside and gets bigger and bigger. The beast needs to be filled, and there's no stopping it now.

I watch as the smoky haze fills the room. My mind swims and swims. I'm gouging. In and out I move between conscious and unconsciousness. Oh, God, at last! How delicious this feels ... Not a worry in the world. I am in my own room, my own hotel – I could be anywhere: New York, Paris, Munich, I could be anyone: a rock star, a painter, an actress ... I have not felt this wonderful in years. All thoughts of my recent troubles – the babies taken, Boy 2 in rehab – recede in the ether of smack and crack and oh my God it's good to be here ... The smoky feel is perfect ... I survey my misty surroundings ... it's so beautiful! The haze, I can hardly see through the blur of it all ... Hang on ... what's that? I look at the carpet. I see something floating – it's my suitcase! Oh my God, what is happening ...? I look closer and then I see it ... it's water. Water everywhere ... The whole floor is floating oh my God, the smoke is steam oh, Jesus! The bath!!!!

I struggle up and wade to the bathroom ... the hot water's been running for three hours and the bath has overflowed into the bedroom – the whole room is in flood. It's a foot deep in water ... Oh, my God!

Needless to say, I'm given my marching orders within the hour. The dismayed manager surveys his destroyed room and tells me there is no possibility of my continuing to stay. He is going to keep the money my brother has paid to try and cover damages. I am told to leave, that I am a liability. Do not to pass 'Go', do not collect R200, go directly to – wherever you come from. Problem is, this time I have nowhere – absolutely no place to go to at all.

And when a junkie's got no place to go, the only logical route seems to walk up the yellow brick road and find a place in any old stable. For me, that place was Hellbrow.

CHAPTER 17

ENTRANCE TO HELL

Yazmean Staggie stumbles down the cobbled streets of Soper Road, two suitcases and a video camera in hand. Dumb donkey slouching to Bethlehem. Green contact lenses stolen from her brother's wife. A red silk yashmak completes her disguise.

She pushes past the swarm of Nigerians, Ghanaians, lounging against the cracked paint hotel pillar walls. The Mountbatten has seen better days; once a top Jo'burg hotel, it is now the home of society's swarms of illegals. Dealers: mercenaries in Ray-Bans, Rolex watches ticking, Nokias and Samsungs a-buzzing, the latest models – they scour the streets, edgy hyaenas looking for business. Corrupt cops cruise the alleys in yellow vans, looking for business. Everybody here is looking for business.

'It's none of your fucking business,' a scabby, homeless whore mutters to no-one in particular.

Yazmean is on a mission. She's a solo agent, she's here to get high. Her camera is generating major focus. Grabbed and pushed as she makes her way up the stairs, the wallflowers pounce on her – new client, prospective sucker, she's a girl – easy target.

'I'll give you one thou for this,' a cool Ghanaian hustles.

'Two – I'll give you two,' a gold-chained, fezzed-up Niger hisses.

'It's not for sale,' seethes Yazmean, pushing past. 'I'm a journalist – it's my work stuff.'

'Journaleeeest,' they chorally mock her.

Beads of sweat gather on her forehead. Withdrawal is setting in, the achy-limbed familiar feeling. She needs a bag of brown badly.

She's travelled far to get to this point – had to shake off the shackles of mommyhood, wifehood, sisterhood, familyhood, and now the red hood covering her face clings to her forehead in sticky sweat.

She has changed everything, no-one knows her here and that's the way she wants it to be …

Her mission is crystal clear. Score some drugs and get these tiresome withdrawal feelings out of the way. Then hook up with some people who want stuff muled to London. Catch a plane, maybe smoke a rock 12 000 feet above sea level, what a plan! Then pick up the drug cash and find a place. Find a publisher, get an advance, write her book, sell her book, be on some great bestsellers' list, make millions of pounds and fuck everyone here back home. She'll show them! But first things first: right now her nose is going drippy drip, she really needs some shit.

From amidst the throng of druggies, slagged out blow-job-skewed-mouth hookers and dealers, a small wiry Hard Livings tattooed coloured man appears.

'Hey, cherry, whatchu got dere? You wan' sum stuff, hey? Lemme introduce you to someone, he's got whatchu want, Room 306. Oh, by the way, the name's Chavon.'

She follows him; there's something about him that she trusts more than the rest, lets him guide her out of the mire of African melting pot madness. She finds herself in a scummy syphilitic lift.

'So I says my name's Chavon. What's yours?'

'Yazmean … Staggie … I'm Yazmean Staggie, the seventh widow of Rashaad – you know, the one that Pagad torched.'

In that moment, in that miniscule moment as I mutter the name of my alter ego, everything changes. No longer the little suburban housewife junkie, middle-class girl who got lost to the clutches of drug hell, I assume an alter ego that is fearsome and she fits me like a snug glove … there is no turning back now: this is who I am … and right now Yazmean's all I've ever wanted to be.

'Staggie!' Chavon embraces her with gusto, does the clenched fist gang 'shake'. She follows suit.

'I'm Hard Livings,' she says with peacock aplomb.

'Me too,' he pulls his T-shirt up to display a faded 'HL' blue tattoo on his scrawny knotty upper arm.

'Howzit, Staggie! Welcome home! Honoured to have you with us.'

The lift shudders to a half-decisive stop. They get out on the third floor. Room 306 winks weirdly at the end of the dank corridor. Her fist is still clenched as Chavon does a scratch-tap-tap code knock on the door.

There's an answering scratch-knock back.

'Jon, issme, me, Chavon. I brought you someone. Open up, Jon ...'

The door opens inchingly slowly. The smell of stale urine overpowers. Orange curtains and the muddy pink ash- and semen-soiled carpet clash like an unwelcome milkshake. Dirty sheets wrinkle forlorn on the single bed in the corner. At the foot of the bed, on the grimy carpet, two bodies lie motionless, like some Parthenon truncated statues.

'Are they dead?' wonders Staggie.

In the corner a black-leathered, punk-looking Nigerian stands legs astride, arms crossed. Behind him the neon light of Ponte flashes on and off. His pointy leather shoes glisten, spotless. He looks like a mean cowboy out of Africa. With the. arrival of a new person, the two bodies slide to attention.

The punk cowboy looks slowly at Yazmean.

'What is it that you want?' he asks, deep staccato bark.

'I need some rocks and some brown,' she says. 'I don't have cash, but I will tomorrow. Cheque's going to clear. Can I put this down as a deposit?'

She opens up the 30 grand video camera. 'It's worth a lot of money. It's my life. I'm not selling it.'

He inches forward, picks up the state-of-the-art equipment. Puts it down, disinterested.

'This is a piece of shit … but because you seem like you are lost, I will hold it and give you drugs for R600. Here. The name's Jon. Jon Bosco, and don't you forget it.'

He takes out 12 rocks.

'Here. Smoke it. You bring the cash, I give you back the camera. I don't want it, it's a piece of shit.'

The cowboy motions to Chavon to take the camera; he obeys his master like a circus monkey, carrying the gadget into the small adjoining room.

Yazmean doesn't notice, she's too busy surveying her spoils. She hasn't seen a stash like this for a long, long time. For so long she's been treated like some sad stray, with scraps and titbits and leftovers.

'Heaven must be heaven' plays in her head. She kneels at the little brown table, she opens the plastic housing the rock. A glass pipe and a lighter miraculously appear. Chavon joins her. The two other occupants slide in closer, gracious hosts. They are fixed on her spoils. Lounge lizards, they wait, hopeful for a scrap. She doesn't notice as the young coloured whore Shamilla unzips her suitcase and starts rummaging through her things.

The BIC lighter flicks to attention. Her hit is loaded. It's all systems go now. Lift off lift off we have a lift off. The crack and sizzle of bicarb and cocaine fill the silent night. She closes her eyes, she zooms right out the room

... she's high flying now ... so high ... She loads another and another. Hungry, hungry girl, that hole gets bigger. Generous Leonine, she breaks off pieces and hands them to the hyaenas who pant and watch.

She smokes ... she zooms she spins she flies, gets rocked up high so high out of her little brain that's become so provincial. Everything spins and blurs, spins and blurs, her heartbeats hit 300 now. Sizzle crack sizzle crack the cocaine burns on metal gauzes, drips down crack glass pipes. BIC flames cast eerie shadows on the smutty wall.

She is a comfort to these strangers. They kneel before her, grateful congregation. Benevolent priestess. It is a holy communion.

'Hey hey my my rock and roll will never die it's better to burn out than to fade away hey hey ...' Neil Young crackles in the background on the little radio that some junkie or other has pawned for a hit.

While Yazmean's been smoking, she has not noticed Chavon and his honcho, the razor wire-scarred Armin, carrying all her belonging into the adjoining room, where Shamilla rifles through it like some Lolita looter picking out this, that and everything her whorish little heart desires.

————————————

The rocks are gone, smoked up into the ether. A sorry heap of torn plastic lies haplessly on the little wooden table. Now

all four occupants of 306 are on their hands and knees.
Like experts in Braille, they search the table, the carpet in
hope of a scrap, a tiny little piece that has fallen. A crumb,
anything... the spun out post-coke air strangulates. On their
knees to the God of Crack, they scour for a forgotten rock.
A breadcrumb, a grain of sugar, anything white or yellow,
anything. A piece of bread is burnt on the pipe. It smells
like toast in here.

Jon Bosco watches from the window. His arms crossed,
he surveys his territory like an oil tycoon.

Yazmean is spun out. She can't bear it. She needs some
down thing, some smack to come down and ease the strung-
out feeling.

Cocaine-bold, she saunters to Bosco.

'Gimme some heroin, you motherfucking Nigerian pimp!'
all brazen-like.

Thwack! She's felled, smacked to the ground. She feels her
jawbone split on impact. She holds her stinging face. Two
tears plop out her dark-pupilled, cracked-out eyes.

'Don't ever say that word in my house again,' he says,
sadistic smile. He walks out. Slams the door. She hears the
key turn. They're locked in.

Her new family circles her, hyaena happy, accusingly
triumphant. Oh, God, what's going on? Where is this place
and who are these people?

'I need to go to the loo,' she whispers.

———————————

And in true *Ripley's Believe It Or Not* fashion, or perhaps like the miraculous light that bolted unsavoury Saul to become pleasant Paul on the road to Damascus, Jon B's unexpected thwack to my left jaw somehow completely and utterly lifted my desire to ever imbibe another hit of heroin. In an unconscious serendipitous fashion, he well and truly smacked it right out of me. Unfortunately, my hunger for crack more than made up for my new-found abstention.

———————

'I said I need to go to the loo.' I'm starting to flip out in this room. Yazmean's gone for now. No energy left for alter egos I just want to get out of here. Maybe call and beg my brother to let me in, get one more chance. I can't be here any longer.

'Did you hear me?'

'Ssshtttt …' says Chavon.

Chavon is standing behind the curtain peeping onto the street below. His paranoia is extreme. Every move anyone makes he darts a killer look.

'OK, listen, I'm going …'

I go to the door, it's locked. Jon Bosco took the key. We're locked in.

'I said I'm – '

'Shut the fuck up, Staggie!!' Chavon comes in close and grabs my arm.

'I need to use the fucking toilet, OK!?' I hiss, trying to break free.

'You can't go in there, Jon Bosco said!' Shamilla's hot breath licks at my ears.

'Well, then, I am gonna wee right here,' I say, triumphant.

'It's OK, let her go, I will watch her,' says Chavon.

Shamilla glares, little usurped vixen.

Yazmean sits on the loo trying to not to let her backside touch the seat. Aids VD syphilis is all she thinks of. She finds it hard to pee while Chavon's eyes drill into her. From the corner of her eyes she catches sight of something on a tile … from where she's sitting it looks like a huge rock. She becomes fixated on the possibility.

'I haven't got all fucking night, Staggie – do your thing. Don't fuck with me,' says Chavon.

His foot is right next to the rock. Oh, God, if he moves he's going to crush it. She smiles at him trying to distract him.

'Gimme a blow job, Staggie.' He leers at her.

Still no pee.

He moves in closer undoing his zip, holds his weeny little wrinkled cracked-out penis. 'Hey, did you hear me?'

It comes, wee gushes out at last.

'Fuck you,' she says pulling up her tights.

'Wouldn't mind that,' he sniggers.

She pulls the chain.

She brushes past him, bends down and swoops up her rock she's fixated on. Fuck! It's a half-sucked peppermint.

She stalks back to where Shamilla's sulking. Chavon is **her** man – what's that white bitch been doing with him?

Chavon heads back to the window and stares out onto the deserted alley.

'I got a bad feeling,' he says. 'I think they coming.'

'Who?' says Yazmean.

'Shhh – !' say Chavon and Shamilla in unison …

Chavon pushes a bookshelf against the door. Chairs and a table follow. They watch his every move.

Chavon turns the lights off. They sit in darkness, barricaded in. Every now and then the Coca-Cola neon Ponte sign casts a red light into the tiny room. On off on off. Modern-day Tower of Babel, concrete monstrosity.

Somewhere in the night they fall asleep. Three strangers stretched out, curled up against each other on a single bed. The night yawns itself to sleep. Snuffed out.

A week later she's still there. On her hands and knees.

CHAPTER 18

BOERE BLITZ

BANG CRASH DUSH BANG CRASH!!!!!

Sunday 5 am, Mountbatten Hotel. The narcotics squad seizes the building. It's an army-like operation. Each floor is sealed off; the entire block is cordoned off by Casspirs. Yellow vans flashing red lights, screaming sirens wake the tired inner city from its drugged out sleep. A big Boer blitz is on.

Simultaneously one, two, three doors are kicked in, in one well-timed action. Nigerian dealers are truncheoned awake. White narcs swarm everywhere. Passports, cash, drugs, electrical appliances, CD players, TVs, video machines, cellphones are seized.

THE PIRATES OF THE LAW HAVE COME TO PLUNDER. Nigerians' heads smashed to the floor, whores' frail bodies flung against walls. Blood dripping down the noses of great blubbering black men, begging for mercy. The yells and moans of felled warriors playing out like some spastic melody. *Sjamboks* beat out dizzy rhythms on great broad black backs.

No-one is arrested. This is new law. Kangaroo kind. This is operation Fuck You. Code name: Plunder. Mission: Steal.

The lawmen strut out whistling goose-stepping. The vehicles roll out into the Sunday morning like slimy mercury. The cops go back to their wives, their lives. They call it Crime Stop.

—————————————

Yazmean is shell-shocked from the raid. She's not used to this brutality. She longs to go home to her family, her little picket fence life in the North West province, her home, her children, her percolator, her husband, her sick holey suicidal dream. Then she remembers she doesn't have one. A family, or a home. Nowhere to rest her weary body, her weary bones. She's here press sticked to hell. She gives Jon Bosco her wedding ring for a rock, she'll get it back soon, tomorrow, whenever, but right now she needs to get loaded.

—————————————

Two weeks later I'm still in Room 306. I can't leave. Maybe it's the crack, maybe it's the scintillating company I'm keeping. There's something about this little pocket of people. I'm drawn in, fascinated by this underbelly of darkness. It feels like after all this time teetering on the edge of middle-class neurosis, at last my protected whiteness is being sullied and marked with some criss-cross scars of real life. *'You're doing this as research for the novel. So enjoy the ride,'* the voice tells me. The voice is back! The voice keeps me company and urges me to stay every time I think of packing it all in and leaving. *'Stay,'* it tells me. *'This is the real deal. Fuck everyone.'*

CHAPTER 19

KNOCKING

'Do you actually fuck them?' Yazmean is standing with Shamilla on Soper Road, the red light avenue in Hillbrow, amongst the throng of hookers sullenly showing their wares. Tears in their laddered stockings unify the string of glaring whores. Black, white, coloured, yellow, pink, they come in all shapes and sizes, all ages.

'Naaa. Are you mad?' laughs Shamilla. 'We just knock them. You know, take their cash.'

Cars snail past, hungry men looking for dirty sex.

'You see, you gotta knock them, else what you gonna do? Fuck them? Take their cash, promise them the sex and then fuck off as soon as you can, that's the only way,' explains the 15-year-old, ancient woman. Yazmean doesn't want to show that she feels like a little green bunny hopping up and down, not sure what burrow she can crawl into here.

An old Mediterranean man snails past for the fifth time.

'What the fuck you want? Are you window-shopping, Mister?' Shamilla shouts. He stops. Reverses.

'Watch here,' she grins. She talks to him through his window. She gets in. The car drives off. Now Yazmean is all alone, without an ally. She feels like a very, very big red sore thumb in her long-sleeved jersey, military trousers and

good old Docs. The winter air bites and pulls at her ears.
She flags down a cab, can't stay here.
Yazmean heads for Bob's Bar. 'Maybe I'll find friends there.
Get away from the street,' she thinks to herself.

_____

She doesn't. Find a friend. 'I don't think I have any left. I
am all I have and absolutely alone in this world. It's what
I have been craving for years. It feels kind of cool – empty,
but cool,' she tells herself. Somewhere in the night at Bob's
Yazmean does meet someone, though: Scaly Frank. When
you're an addict, you unfortunately don't have very good
taste in men ...

_____

SCENE: INT. LATE NIGHT. BOB'S BAR.

YAZMEAN and **FRANK** sit on a fluorescent couch
watching fish swim in a tank. The bar is
almost empty. They are very drunk. A dwarf
singer sings the same song over and over as
if looped in a bad karaoke machine.

YAZMEAN

I'd really like a house made of walls of
goldfish one day. Like a fish tank. You
know, the whole structure would be made
of bullet-proof glass, so no robbers could
break in. And all these fish would be

swimming round and round. About this thick.
(She indicates half a metre.) Maybe a shark
or two.

FRANK

You wanna come home with me? You're a
helluva intelligent and interesting girl,
you know. I'm pretty choosey who I invite
home with me. I don't just go for anyone.

YAZMEAN

Well, since there's no one else here … *(she
giggles)* … I'll come home with you on one
condition …

FRANK

Condoms? Hey, if that's what turns you on,
I'm cool, safe sex no problemo.

YAZMEAN

You build me a fish-walled house.

FRANK

No problemo.

YAZMEAN

But first you must buy me some rocks. A
huge pile.

                    FRANK
For the house?

                    YAZMEAN
No, man. *(Laughs.)* To smoke. Come.

They leave…

SCENE: INT. NIGHT. FRANK'S HOUSE. TROYEVILLE.

FRANK'S house is seedy. Although it has
some yuppy appliances, it has a distinct
bachelor unkempt feel. Smelly cat litter is
in the corner. Dirty dishes and clothes are
strewn everywhere.

YAZMEAN sits at a table laden with debris
and bottles. She happily loads herself a
big hit of crack. **FRANK** enters in a dressing
gown; he wants some action.

                    FRANK
God, you look sexy in that light, you know,
with that pipe in your mouth, like that
chick from *Pulp Fiction*.

YAZMEAN ignores him, she is totally
concentrating on enjoying her drugs.

FRANK

This is a sex drug, isn't it? *(LONG BEAT)*
Hey, let me try some.

YAZMEAN looks irritated as she gives him a
tiny piece. She watches him and immediately
takes the pipe back and loads another for
herself. **FRANK** puts some R&B on.

FRANK

I don't usually like black music, but one
thing they know how to do is make good
fuck rhythms.

FRANK sways to the music. He watches **YAZMEAN,**
putting his hands down his pants. She does
not see him - she is fixated on smoking.

SCENE: INT. NIGHT LATER. FRANK'S LOUNGE.

It is later. **YAZMEAN** has finished with the
rocks and is now scraping the pipe. The
sound of a metal clip rasping on the glass
is irritating **FRANK**. He's been waiting for
sex for over two hours and his patience has
run out.

FRANK
(walking up and down)
C'mon, I'm sure it's finished. It's fucking
rude to do that while I just sit and wait
for you!

YAZMEAN
So don't. Do something. Get a life. Go to
bed. Go out. *(BEAT)* I want to get more.

FRANK
You must be fucking insane! That's it. I've
spent over 500 bucks on you. I'm putting the
lights off and we're going to bed.

YAZMEAN *continues to scrape.* **FRANK** *picks up
the pipe and smashes it in the sink.*

SCENE: INT. NIGHT. FRANK'S BEDROOM.

YAZMEAN is lying at the bottom of the bed,
curled up in a foetus-like ball, her back
to **FRANK.** He is naked and trying to enter
YAZMEAN from behind. He rubs and rubs himself
against her, breathing heavily. Her eyes are
wide and she is frozen to his touch. This
goes on and on until **FRANK** pushes himself
on top of her and forces himself into her.
YAZMEAN looks totally removed, her head

turned sideways looking at the wall as **FRANK** thrusts into her.

SCENE: EXT. DAWN. ROAD TO HILLBROW.

The sky is anew and turning a gorgeous pink as **YAZMEAN** walks up Nugget Hill leading like the yellow brick road up into Hillbrow. The birds begin to sing and the city begins to wake. Peace reigns. The song of the birds becomes more intense, the beautiful concerto crescendos into a cacophony of squawking screeches. **YAZMEAN** coughs intermittently as she walks.

Blood! There's blood everywhere. As I walk through the door of 306, I'm greeted by a room upturned in chaos. It's all in a heap of a mess, except for one corner where Chavon is sitting loading rocks onto a pipe. It's as though he's not part of the scene. Then I see her, Shamilla, paper-pale: she's not moving, her head is matted, caked in blood. Oh my fuck! I think she's dead.

'What the fuck – ?' I say to Chavon. 'What happened here? Is she – what happened?'

I finally managed to get Chavon to tell me.

Shamilla tried to steal from Jon B's stash in the bathroom. He caught her, beat the crap out of her, held her out the window and threatened to throw her in the alleyway. To silence her screams, he broke a chair on her head.

'And now she's jus' laying there. But she'll be OK – she got a hard head,' says Chavon, breathing out a pile of smoke.

'I think you should take her to a hospital, a doctor, see if she's OK,' I say.

He ignores me.

I pick up what's left of my things and walk out. Shamilla's wearing a pair of my favourite tights.

I've really got no clue what to do now, no cash, no place to stay. And so when in doubt, when you've got nowhere to go, go home. But I don't have a home ... so I decide to go to the closest thing to home – and that's my brother's place. I need cash badly. I have nothing. I arrive at the Parktown residence; my brother and his wife are at work. Great – no-one here, besides the maid.

'I have left a few things here, I just need to pick them up,' I say to her as I slide into the huge wooden-floored house.

I take a sports bag and start loading things I think I'll be able to move. A phone, some clothes, a camera, a dictaphone ... baby's toys. The Nigers will want this shit, I think. I turn back, see an enormous silver knife glinting in the open drawer. I pick it up. A weapon! That's what I need – or, at the very least, I'm sure some Nigerian will love it.

In 20 minutes I'm all geared up and back on the road. As I walk towards the main drag, where I will catch a mini bus taxi to Hillbrow, I spot three men crowded around a black beaten-up car. As I walk past, a small wiry young man says: 'Hey, where you going? You need a lift?'

'Where are you going?' I ask.

'We're off to the 'Brow. You want a lift?'

'Sure,' I say, 'that's where I'm going. Sure.' Now I don't have to spend cash on taxi fare. More drugs for me. Great!

We've got car trouble: the car breaks down twice before we get to Abel Road. I'm beginning to wonder whether saving some cash on a taxi has been worth it ... but, hey, now we're here and all I've got to do is get out of this car, leave the dicks behind and go and swop some of my brother's stuff for a whole lot of gear. Party time!

Thwack!

The car behind us crashes into us.

'No, man, fuck it, no!' says Baby Face, a scar-faced specimen. Paul, the lanky dark Niger, jumps out to survey the damage,

The man in the car behind is a round, pot-bellied coloured man. 'Hey, *jissus*, I'm sorry, really – I think I saw the light change and I thought youse was pulling off. Really sorry.'

The Niger and the scarface gather in a whispered huddle, conferring on their next move.

'Listen here,' says Baby Face. 'You know, we can't just leave this. We need some compensation – we're not insured. We need something for the damages.'

'*Ja*, my *broer*, I understand – problem is, I don't have any cash on me ... my wife has got it all.'

'So where's your wife?' asks Baby Face.

'She's at Bruma Lake; she works there on a Wednesday,' says Mr Accident.

'Sweet, let's go.'

The mission to Bruma Lake is a debacle. I wait in the car and watch them for what seems like hours haggling with the man's wife, who doesn't seem to want to know a damn thing about her husband's problems. On and on they go. I really wish I'd never gotten into this fucking car. Tsepo, the young Sowetan gangster, sits in the front rifling through the things in my bag that I've stolen from my brother. I don't notice that he's already ripped almost all the valuables out of there.

'C'mon!' I shout from the car. 'Let's get a fucking move on!' They ignore me. I see the knife glistening from the sports bag. I clutch it. It's a huge, butcher-like knife. I feel insane – hanging for crack with a huge dagger in my hand ... I begin to allow my shot split brain to formulate a plan ... I am going to jump out of the car wielding the knife, screaming at the man and his wife, threatening them, until they give us the cash ... I will cast them into a state of terror. I can't stop thinking of doing this ... one two three, it's all systems go now ... Just as I open the door and do my *Scream 2* impersonation, Baby Face and Paul turn back and head towards the car.

Baby Face is clutching R500 in his hand.

'C'mon, let's get the fuck outta here and go smoke! We've been riding around, fucking wasting time for over four hours now.'

'C'monnnnnnn, let's go!!!' I screech.

I'm given nothing.

I'm watching them sizzle the rocks and smoke the crack and I am ignored and given nothing!!!! Oh my God!!! I can't believe this. It's dark now and we're holed up in the shitty Hillbrow Inn and these motherfuckers are ignoring my plaintive cries.

'Listen here, I really, really need a hit!' I implore Paul the Niger. 'I have been with you guys all day and I can't take it anymore. Pleaaaaassssseeee give me some!'

Finally a third of a rock is broken off and grudgingly handed to me. 'Smoke,' says Baby Face as though he is giving me a cricket ball of the stuff. Oh my God, this is much worse than smoking with Boy 2. It's the first time I have thought of my husband in weeks ...

'So how 'bout we go and do a bit of H and B? Maybe go to that larney house that you were leaving from when we met you this morning.' Baby Face is lighting my rock and holding the lighter flame for me. It feels like he wants to torch me.

'What's H and B?' I ask after I've blown out the much-needed smoking rush.

'House-breaking, baby. Let's go house-break your family. Hey, whatchu say?'

We can't do that. No, not even in my near-psychotic state. I just don't feel right about taking these thugs to my brother's place – after all, he's the only one who's given two continental fucks about my well-being ...

'Naa,' I say. 'They got a dog. I don't wanna go there.'

'Well, then, who else? Come on, think. You must know lots of larneys.'

Then suddenly it's clear as a crystal little bell.

Frank, that slimy mother cocksucker. Frank from Bob's Bar! Yeah!

'OK,' I say. 'I've got someone. In fact, he's not even that far away from here ... let's go ... let's go now and visit Frank.'

SCENE: EXT. LATE NIGHT. FRANK'S HOUSE.
TROYEVILLE.

A beaten-up old car pulls up in front of
FRANK'S house. **YAZMEAN, BABY FACE, TSEPO**
and **PAUL** get out, silently. All the men are
armed. **BABY FACE** does a gangsta-type fist
salute to **YAZMEAN,** they all follow suit.
YAZMEAN fixes her red scarf-like yashmak

around her head and walks up the darkened
steps leading to the front door. **YAZMEAN**
knocks loudly. Nothing. She tries again.
No response.

YAZMEAN

Frank! Frank! Open the door. Please, it's
me! Open! *(Nothing)*

She bangs louder.

YAZMEAN

(acting)

Frank! Frank, you gotta help me. I'm hurt.
Please, Frank. I need you. Please help me!

She grins at the three men who are waiting
in the dark at the bottom of the stairs,
guns cocked. **BABY FACE** does a thumbs-up. A
passage light flicks on. The silhouette of
bald **FRANK** can be seen approaching the door.

FRANK

What the fuck do you want? It's three in the
morning. Get the fuck away from my house or
I'm calling the cops!

YAZMEAN

Listen, I'm in trouble. I need some money.
There's a cab waiting - he won't go unless
he gets money. I need 300 bucks.

FRANK

(walking away from door)

Fuck you, you stupid bitch!

BABY FACE

(hissing)

Yazmean, try harder! Say something else!
Don't let him go!

YAZMEAN

Frank, please, I've got nowhere else to go!
(Fakes crying) I've been raped. I need to go
to the hospital. Please!

FRANK slips a R50 note under the door.

FRANK

Now get off my property, you cunt!

YAZMEAN hears the word and something snaps. She indicates to **BABY FACE** to shoot **FRANK.** **BABY FACE** hesitates. **YAZMEAN** leaps down the stairs and struggles to get the gun herself. The lights in the house go off. The chance to kill **FRANK** is over.

SCENE. INT. NIGHT. CAR.

YAZMEAN is fighting furious. She coughs. The car is driving dangerously fast back to Hillbrow.

YAZMEAN

Why didn't you let me shoot him? His head was right there. I had a perfect shot. You guys are losers, you know that!? A bunch of scared fucking babies! I'm used to professionals. Hard Livings. The Staggies. I can't believe what a bunch of losers I hooked up with!

———————

We find ourselves back in the 'Brow, in a dingy one-bedroomed flat on Soper Road. Once again I'm offered nothing for my efforts. Once again I watch as these dickheads smoke their crack. Then, like a very bad movie, the day comes to an end and my life unfolds in an ugly detour – a turn very much for the worse, all in very slow motion.

———————

I've got a gun in my mouth. I don't know much about guns, but the taste of metal makes me want to gag …

'Open your legs,' a surly, scar-faced specimen called Baby Face instructs me. I'm huddled in a frozen ball, my hands press my knees together.

'Please don't rape me … '

CHAPTER 20

SHEEP WITHOUT GRASS

It's a day after the rape. I've been in the 'Brow for three weeks now. I've lost 12 kilograms. Unlike the Beverly Hills diet, on the Hillbrow Diet you eat: nothing! Hey, come to the 'Brow, don't eat a single solid, smoke as much crack as you can. Takes away all appetite and when you can, drink a few gulps of tea, made in some syphilitic bed-sit of some syphilitic whore …

I'm beginning to look like an Auschwitz or Serbian girl. When I lie in the bath in some or other hotel room, it aches as my spine touches the enamel bottom; I can feel each bone bruising, pushing back. I think I look fabulous. I have always wanted to be this thin and now I am. 'You can never be too rich or too thin,' my mother used to tell me.

Something happens in my head to me after I'm raped, I just don't care anymore. It's a deep sigh, a deep 'what-the-fuck-who-the-hell-whatever' kind of feeling. It's like every day's a hangover from the one before, from the one before, from the one before. It's a true giving up of all semblance of a normal life. I'm starting to fit in here, find my own place, identity, my own little stitch in the torn fabric of this ghetto.

I do not report the rape. I do not even think about it. After I've smoked with them, I put it all behind me in some faraway sack. It's only later much later – in fact, years on – that I confront any of this.

It's the day after the rape. Ah, I have said that before. It seems everything is seen in my life BR (before rape) and AR (after rape). I guess that's what happens with events that traumatise the human soul. You see everything according to a new frame of reference, a new time line.

I'm sitting on a ledge of a pavement on Abel Road, empty shell, demoralised and defeated. I do not realise it, but I have a raging temperature, having developed some type of 'flu that is more than likely the beginning of pneumonia. I hack and cough like some aged hag on the pavement. I am smoking a fag that I have managed to bum off a passer-by. I have no plans, no itinerary, nowhere to go. I just sit and stare. It is a stare that penetrates everything and thinks nothing at all, that cutting-edge stare that goes into the white noise beyond thought or feeling.

Suddenly a six-foot-tall, dark-haired, long-legged creature appears before me.

'What's wrong baby?' her voice is Eartha Kitt deep and purry. 'My name's Jenna.' Her arm embraces me, shrouds me, warms me. I feel like weeping.

I tell her bits of the jagged sorry tale of my jagged sorry life.

'Hey, you're gonna be OK, everybody's got some or other story, you know. Let me take you to a friend – he's very cool for a Niger, you know. He's got a nice clean spot just here,' she points behind us to the La Rosa Hotel. It's one of the few hotels in 1999 that still resembles a liveable spot. In fact, this one has retained some old-world charm. 'He'll give us something to smoke, make you feel better,' she says.

Like a sheep without grass, I follow her.

_____

We walk up a great gleaming wooden staircase. It's like Tara in *Gone With the Wind*. We get to the third floor and stop at Room 307.

The door opens and there stands a man. He's got a noticeable scar on his left cheek. He's short and stockyish and introduces himself as Goodluck. His name impresses me, it feels like a sign from somewhere, a sign that's telling me my luck's about to change. Jenna and Goodluck go into the adjoining room and leave me, delirious and feverish, on the sofa.

Weeks later I discover that their little *tete-a-tete* entailed Jenna selling me to Goodluck for a handful of crack.

_____

The room is warm, the late afternoon sun streams through – it's the first time I feel safe in ages. My two new friends reappear. Jenna hands me a rock.

'Smoke this. I'll come back later and see how you're doing.'

She disappears in a puff of air, like a fairy godmother. My hacking cough fills the awkward silence that now taunts us, two strangers left in the room together. The coughing doesn't stop.

Goodluck sees how ill I am and immediately urges me to get into bed. For two days I am lost to the world; I have developed a raging fever and my new acquaintance watches me from the bedside, urging me to drink a concoction of whisky and lemon and whatever other medicine he adds. His vigilance pays off and my fever finally breaks. I pull back into the land of living. After four days, like Lazarus I rise.

Goodluck and I become friends. I tell him bits and pieces about myself and he shares how he has come to South Africa the previous year, looking for the whole greener pasture deal. How in Nigeria people talk of this land of milk and honey in the south. He has an electrical engineering degree. He wants to work here as a legal one day, but right now he's trapped in some dive in Ghetto Land, selling crack and trying to make ends meet. This is the sad tale of many of his countrymen.

'Before I arrived here, I was promised a place to stay and that everything would be easily organised – a visa and work permit,' he tells me one evening. 'However, when I got here it was very different. I had no money and no food and I found that my return plane ticket was taken by the man whose address I was given to stay with. Soon I was told to start off by selling some joints. I was only making, say, R20 a day. It was far too little cash to do anything. There were plenty of days when I could only eat bread and drink some tea. Then I was given a few pipes to add to my wares. I made a little more and sometimes I could buy a bit of meat. After a month, the chance to sell the rocks came up and, of course, I jumped on this opportunity. Because when you are hungry, you will do things you might not normally choose to do for money, especially when you are a stranger in a foreign land.'

His words resonate. *I, too, am a stranger in a foreign land ...*

'I hate this life,' he says. 'I hate selling the drugs. I hate seeing the suffering that this poison causes. But I am trapped – I do not know how to escape this cage. I could go back home to Nigeria, but I will arrive with nothing and in my people, the Ibo's eyes, that is a very, very bad, shameful thing for a man to admit – defeat.'

I watch him as he talks, quietly and with dignity, and I get lost in him. We're smoking a joint and the heady feeling lifts me and takes me to a feeling that I thought I had lost long ago in the mire of domesticity and abuse and mewling babies and smack. I feel like my whole life has taken me to this place – to hook up with Goodluck and find the love I am feeling in my heart for him. It's the first pure feeling I have had in years. I am sure he feels the same. It is sweet and tender.

'I would like to take you to Lagos and have you meet my mother,' he says often, stroking my hand or gently moving a stray strand of hair out of my eyes. We spend more and more time sharing ourselves with each other. We are both Leos, almost astrological twins born in the same year, 1966, a day apart. Our connection does not cross to the physical for the first 10 days of my stay. When we finally creep into bed together one night and feel our bodies spoon against each other, and the desire rises, we connect on a plane that is so sweet, I taste it for days after.

I am hardly smoking rocks anymore; he is encouraging me to stop. I am putting on a bit of weight and my coughing has all but subsided. But just as it all looks set to change and me to get healthy and normal for the first time in years, the addict in me emerges full force, comes thundering in, armed to the teeth, pouncing and eager to sabotage the situation.

'I've got no money. Please, just take this pair of jeans and these shoes and give me another rock.'

It's 2 am on a Saturday night in Hillbrow. A junkie is sitting in Goodluck's room begging him for crack. I have been watching the man smoke away his cash, he's even given away his wallet and now he's getting undressed and attempting to swop his clothes for a tiny little rock that will appease him for 10 seconds, and then it will be another and another. It never ends. Soon it will be his car, his house. He will lay them all on this table, looking for that high that will never be found.

Goodluck is too soft-hearted to be a good dealer. I keep telling him to tell the junkies to get lost, but he always tries to treat them with dignity. It's late now and the day is fraying to an end.

'Alright,' he sighs. 'Take this – but it's the last one.'

The junkie sits in his underwear and smokes, pathetic piranha. There is such an empty chasm, a nothingness about him. I know that post-crack feeling so well – when you're at the end of the world and hell is your only wallpaper.

It's freezing outside tonight. It's July mid-winter and Hillbrow is concrete ice.

The junkie finally gets up to leave. He's only wearing socks and grey torn underpants. Goodluck goes into the bedroom and comes back with a pile of clothing.

'Wear this,' he says, giving Mr Naked an old tracksuit left by another desperado. 'And you must wear some shoes. You will freeze tonight.'

He throws a pair of old sneakers down.

'Hurry now, get dressed, we want to sleep.'

The junkie dresses and leaves without a word. Thankless sorry bastard.

'Fuck fuck fuck! No! Oh, fuck, NO!'

I wake to hear Goodluck slamming cupboard doors.

'What's wrong?' I say from bleary lack of sleep.

He's sitting on the edge of the bed, his head in his hands, shaking his head and cursing over and over. At last he looks up.

'The shoes I gave that man last night – those shoes had everything I had in the world! I had R10 000, all the cash I had managed to make since I got out of prison. I put it in the soles of the shoes to be safe there. Oh, God, how can I have been so stupid!? What am I going to do!?'

I sit open-mouthed. I can't believe what he has just told me. He stashed 10 grand in the soles of an old pair of sneakers and then forgot and gave them to that scaggy junkie! What a fucking dumb thing to do!! But I cannot say it; even I – with as little tact as a blind bat – cannot bring myself to say what's on my mind.

I sit in silence, it's like a tomb in Room 307. I try to hold his hand … it seems pointless to say a word, there just seems to be none available to comfort him. Finally:

'Oh my God …' I say. 'Do you think he'll come back?'

Goodluck doesn't answer me. He leaves the room, slamming the door. Oh, God, I search for the whisky that's stashed in the back of the kitchen cupboard. I really need a drink!

Three hours later I hear the key in the door. My heart jumps. He walks in. He looks slightly better. Then he throws a handful of rocks, tightly wrapped in plastic on the table.

'I have managed to get a bit of stock on credit,' he says. 'Fifteen rocks. My brother upstairs helped me out. I suppose the only thing to do is start all over again.'

I haven't smoked a rock in days – Goodluck and I smoke *ganja* all day and every day. It feels as if I have recovered – as if I am no longer an addict! I no longer crave this drug as it lies there in its pathetic glory on the wooden table.

'I've got an idea …' I say slowly. 'You know, I don't wanna smoke this shit ever again. I am so happy with you. I haven't smoked in days. Why don't you let me take 10 of them downstairs and I will sell them for you? It's my way of helping you because you have helped me so much. It will be much safer for me, a white girl, down there than you trying to do it on the street. I'm sure I can do it in under two hours. C'mon, let me do something nice for you, darling.'

Goodluck looks at me; he is dubious for a second, and then I see his face break out in a glorious smile. 'Thank you, that is very thoughtful of you.'

———————

I'm sitting in the public toilets on the third floor, in a cubicle, the door's closed. It's 45 minutes since I left Goodluck to sell his drugs. On the floor in front of me are plastic torn-up wrappers and my little glass crack pipe. It drips inside with liquid crack, it's hardening, turning grey white. I'm looking for something to do a scratch-scrape with. I find a hairclip and start rasping away, scraping the leftovers into a little powdery heap. I load the scrape and smoke it greedily.

I have smoked almost all the rocks. Ten rocks – nearly all gone! All that remains are little pieces of crack crumbs. My heart is pounding 330 beats a minute, I can feel it screaming and thudding at my ribcage like a mad giant, trapped in a castle, bashing to get out.

My eyes are wide shot, cocaine crazy. Dark pupils stare out at nothing, they are enormous. I see myself in the bathroom mirror as I bend down to take a quick sip of water at the basin.

Oh my fuck, what am I going to do …? I have not even made it to the foyer. Something happened an hour back, as I held those rocks, some voice much louder than my own said: *'Why don't you go and smoke a little piece of one, just one and then you can go downstairs and sell the rest?'*

It seemed like a good idea at the time. 'Just one and then I'll go sell the rest,' I told myself. But once I hit that first rock, it was over.

My beasty greedy voice just said *'Yeahhhh!!!'* And there was no stopping that sick monster. Now I'm trying to tie tiny little crumbs of crack together with the bitten, frayed pieces of plastic, trying to come up with ten packets.

'Ten green bottles hanging on the wall, ten green bottles hanging on the wall, and if one green bottle should accidentally fall there'll be nine green bottles hanging on the wall …' the voice whistles as I sweat at my impossible task. It's pathetic!

And now I think of dear Goodluck. How am I going to possibly face him? What am I going to tell him? Oh, God, I can't go back into the room. I can't. I can't.

An hour later I'm still sitting on the floor, scraping away at the jagged-edged little crack pipe. Like some psychotic woodpecker, I peck and scratch. I'm too paranoid and terrified to move.

'What's this – ?'

I stand in front of Goodluck like an errant schoolgirl. He surveys his spoils and looks terribly confused.

'What is the meaning of this?' he asks again, looking at me hard and long.

'I ... smoked ... a ... little bit,' I say. I look down.

He opens each packet, counts what's left of the rocks one by one. Two of his brothers, his fellow Nigerians, are watching a soccer match on the sofa. Nigeria *versus* Ghana. They turn down the volume, preferring to watch this little drama unfold. How is this white girl going to explain herself ...? Ha!

'A bit?' He looks incredulous. 'I don't think so. *All*. You smoked it *all*. Say it!'

'I smoked it ... most of it,' I whisper.

THWACK! He smacks me! Good and hard, right across the face. And again: THWACK!

'Now put some clothes on, some of these. Here. It's time you started working. Paying for your keep. Doing what I bought you for. Ha! You didn't know that, did you? When you came that day – I paid your 'friend' with a pile of crack. So now you must work. Do you hear me!?'

It feels like he is showing off in front of his brothers now, taking control of me ... He pulls a skimpy mini-dress out the cupboard and a pair of tatty stockings.

'And what am I supposed to do with this?' I am still trying to process the fact that he now owns me.

'You must go out there and earn some money, make up for this, what you have done. I am tired of all you fucking addicts. It's over! The days that I am nice Goodluck are over! Now it's *my* turn to be a motherfucker. Go bath now and dress!'

'I won't go out there,' I whinge. 'I'm tired, I want to rest.'

'Well, if you won't go out there and work, then you must leave. You cannot stay here.'

With that Goodluck picks me up, opens the front door and dumps me in the carpeted passage.

I sit for a minute not believing what has just happened. Thrown out yet again – it is the story of my life.

'Baby, I'm sorry,' I moan between the crack of the door and floor. I scratch and knock, on and on. 'Please let me in, please, please. I'm sorry. Baby? Please! I will do whatever you say,' I lie.

The door opens a miniscule crack.

'You better not be lying to me. Come in, there is someone downstairs who's coming up. He wants to smoke and he wants a woman.'

'Oh my God, no!!!' I screech as I see the state of the 'man who wants a woman''s dick. It's tiny, black and shrivelled up. He's an Israeli called Eli and he's taken me into Goodluck's bathroom to suck him off after we have smoked copious amounts of crack. There is something definitely not OK with this man's member.

'No, no, *no*!' I wail. Goodluck knocks and runs in.

'What is wrong with you!? Are you crazy?'

'I won't – I can't – I am not touching that!'

Eli is embarrassed, he stands there naked holding his pock-marked, shrivelled cock.

'This woman is crazy, give me back my dollar!' he blurts.

'Look here,' hisses Goodluck, taking me out the bathroom. 'You cannot behave like this. This is a client, he has been paying me good money – American dollars – and now you start shouting like a crazy person. Why can't you just be quiet, be like a normal woman and do your job?'

'I won't ever!' I yell. 'Don't you understand, I'm not a fucking hooker and I will never touch something like that! I love you. Please forgive me. Can't we go back to the way things were? I don't want to touch another man. I only want you.'

'You must leave now. I gave you a chance, but you say yourself you cannot do this work. You are a lazy, no-good white woman. Go. Now. This time do not come back. This time it is for good.'

Goodluck doesn't shout, he's just tired and empty. This time I don't put up a fight. I'm tired and empty too.

I slowly walk to the door, I feel like crying. I close it behind me. I'm in the passage, I look up and down. There is nowhere to go. I slide down the wall and sit on the carpet outside his door. An hour later I scratch quietly. 'Please can I come in? I will try to be good. Please.'

Silence fills that long corridor. It aches. The door stays closed.

CHAPTER 21

SHIFTING GOAL-POSTS

'Give me a blow job.'

I am in Room 212, the floor below Goodluck's room. Abachu, an enormous Nigerian, has his huge dick in one hand and a rock in another. 'C'mon, you say you want to smoke – well, I want some suck.'

I have been lying and moaning outside Goodluck's door for almost two days and nights and at the end of the second I finally give up and decide to show some initiative and move downstairs.

I really want to smoke and I really don't want to suck this motherfucker's cock, but I'm beginning to weigh up the situation. And when a girl needs some crack, she does things she doesn't want to do. As simple as that. I'm sure that's how most of the hookers land up doing what they do. I doubt many women wake up one day and say: 'Ooh, you know, I would really like to be a hooker on the streets in Hillbrow. I would like to leave my nice, cushy job and my sweet, loving family and go and suck cock and sleep with filthy ugly men for a living.'

'I came here 'cos I had nowhere else to go. Soon I was smoking crack to take away my bad memories of my stepfather, who used to fuck me and beat me up,' says Lerato, a 14-year-old whore from Soweto. She's sitting, cross-legged, on the floral bedspread of the single bed in Abachu's room. She 'works' for Abachu. 'Then, when I was hungry enough and hanging hard enough for a rock, I slept with the first steamer who came my way. Now this is what I do – and you know what? I don't really give a fuck.'

Her friend – Abachu's other girl, Amanda, a 19-year-old skinny coloured girl from Cape Town – comes into the room, out of breath, cash in hand from a quick blow job in some steamer's car. She boasts the same sorry story, escaping abuse, getting hooked on crack and buttons and doing sex work for a living.

These are the first two girls I connected with and 'befriended'. They both ripped me blind – each time I fell asleep I would find I had fewer and fewer clothes in my suitcase when I woke up – but ultimately they became like big little sisters to me, filling the need for a family in the hell-hole in which we had all found ourselves. It seemed in some screwed-up way we were looking out for each other.

I kept insisting: 'I'm not a hooker. I won't go on the street.' But one night, having not eaten for two days and not able to beg and connive yet another hit off someone else's well-earned crack pipe, I could see no other way but to venture downstairs and onto Soper Road.

That night, I hooked up with a woman called Sylvia, who was once a nice Jewish girl from somewhere in the northern suburbs. A few years back she had fallen foul of her family and had found herself with a serious crack addiction. She was about 30, although in bad light she looked closer to a pock-marked 50. She, too, had a sorry story to tell about how she got there and how she was trying to get enough cash to visit her kids. Problem was, every time she made some, she smoked it all away. She suggested we hang out together, and do one man between the two of us. 'They love it with two girls. Y'know, we don't have to *do* anything – we just play around, you know, we're not going to have sex … we just *act* sexy and get him to buy us plenty rocks.'

The 'him' we chose turned out to be a counsellor, who now worked at the rehab I had been to, back in '96. No kidding. I imagined that after hearing all these addicts' stories of Hillbrow and crack and seedy hotels, curiosity had got the better of him and now he was caught in a cycle of addictive behaviour himself.

We took him upstairs into Sylvia's room. We got him to buy R400 of crack. We took off our tops and, bare-breasted, we smoked and nuzzled against each other. We turned out the lights and created a sexy atmosphere with candlelight and as we smoked our crack, we intermittently played with each other in the mirror while he watched. He was turned on for sure. We never had to do more than that … We giggled and laughed and flirted with him and manipulated him to buy us another R300 worth of rocks. And then we told him we were going to get another girl and we left him there, hard-cocked and stranded. We ran off into the ink black night, giggling, looking for our next victim to knock.

I saw him once when I went to visit that rehab, in 2001, two years after I cleaned up. I don't think he could quite place me as the thieving hooker who came close to doing a threesome with him in some dingy whore hotel, but I did get the feeling he was pretty happy to say goodbye when I left after sharing my drug-and-clean-up story.

That was the first real 'trick' I did, and as far as jobs went, it wasn't that bad … it seemed so easy then, too good to be true. Which, of course, it was.

Oh my God, she's bleeding to death!

I walk into Abachu's room and Lerato is kneeling on the floor next to Amanda. Amanda is paper-white. She looks like she is hardly conscious.

Oh my God, what has happened?

Amanda has been stabbed in the vagina by two men who have taken her up onto the Yeoville Ridge and fucked her and then had fun with her with a broken, jagged-edged beer bottle.

'Black Label, a quart,' she mutters. She needs to get to a hospital, she needs help, that's for sure. Abachu calls a cab and organises a South African girl to accompany her to casualty. Two days later Amanda is back on the street. There's no time for convalescence, the call of the crack pipe is true miracle medicine.

For me, the goal-posts keep getting shifted. First I say: 'I am not a hooker' – that I will not do any of this sex stuff for crack. Then I play with Sylvia and that does not seem so bad. Next I do a dealer, then another and then another. Now it's midnight on a Thursday, the wind is icy, blowing me this way and that. I am wearing a tiny mini-skirt, tattered tights and I look like any other girl on the street looking to do a trick. I get in a car that's snailed past twice. He's an Indian man, not bad-looking, called Sadam. He takes me to his palatial home in Lenasia. He pays me R100. He fucks me on his wife's bed, she's away visiting her mother. I see a picture of them at their Muslim wedding. 'She's pretty,' I say.

As we leave, I steal a cellphone. Maybe it's hers. He takes me back to Hillbrow. I swop the phone for four rocks, buy two more with the R100. An hour later I am back on the street. I need more. And that's the way it goes. Shifting goal-posts inch by inch until the field's wide, wide open.

CHAPTER 22

FIVE WEEKS

I've been here for five weeks now. I'm getting hungrier by the day. Now there's no difference between me and the faceless bony hookers who sell their wares on Abel or Soper Road. My education, my upbringing count for nothing here. The hunger grows and the hole in my soul gets bigger and blacker. I hardly ever think of my old life anymore: it's like some far-off coastal seaside dream, with merry-go-rounds, pink milkshakes and pony rides. Another life. My husband, my babies, my home, my maid, my family have become misty memories stored in some distant cauldron of once was. They sometimes find their way into my dreams, sometimes I wake and I feel like I am weeping, but I sort that out soon enough with a hit of a pipe. Sucking the devil's cock, that's what they call it. That pipe can make you forget everything.

One strung-out Sunday evening, I con a taxi driver into taking me to Parkhurst, a yuppie suburb in the north. I have been told a couple of days back by an old junkie connection, who came into the 'Brow to score, that Boy 2 attends Narcotics Anonymous meetings there with inmates from his rehab every Sunday night.

I am bone-hungry, on a mission to get money off my cash cow husband and I tell the driver to wait as I trundle towards the recreation hall, two suitcases weighing me down like that dumb Bethlehem donkey.

The meeting has already begun. The ultra-violet lights and the scrubbed-clean faces of about 100 recovering addicts all but blind me as I stumble in.

I find a chair in a circle. People are introducing themselves – 'Hi, my name's Dave and I'm an addict'; 'Hi, I'm Marie – I'm an addict' – and so it goes. Then the circle gets to me. I say: 'My name is Yazmean Staggie, and I'm a member of GOD – Gangstas On Drugs.' I giggle. Someone on the other side laughs loudly. There! I have made my entrance and now everyone knows who I am!

Now I twitchingly scout the room ... Oh my God! I can hardly believe that the well-rounded, healthy-looking guy I spot, sitting across the room next to the squeaky-clean blonde, is my husband! There is no time to register the blurred emotions coursing through me – they might be fury. They might be envy. They might even be about the pain of betrayal. All I am aware of is a rush of rage, followed by an impulse that is venal, violent revenge.

Without a second thought, I get up. The chair screeches. 'I really need some money!' I bark, my eyes scream at him. Not 'Hello, dear husband, how are you?' No '*Hi, honey, I'm home*' moment here ...

He is horribly embarrassed. He pulls the hood of his sweatshirt over his head. He wants to sink into the tiled floor. Like Peter, he denies me over and over.

'Do you hear me? I said I'm hungry! I'm fucking starving!! I have got nothing! I'm so hungry, and you are so *fat!!*' I wail, cracked-out ho.

He pulls the hood further down. Denied again ... that damn cock just doesn't stop crowing. I look around me – they are all staring at me ... I grab my luggy suitcases, burst into tears and fall out into the icy dark night, crouch on the tennis court and rack-sob my heart out.

Someone appears at my side.

'I need a drink. I need to get to a bar. Will you take me to Bob's? You know Bob's Bar?' I sob, snot laced with crack gumming my nostrils. My hands are shaking.

The stranger takes me there. That taxi driver never waited.

It's a pale wintry morning. I have the last remnants of my clothes in a bag, which some hooker wants to swop me for a rock. I stand on the stairs of La Rosa. This is my home now. It almost feels like I have never been anywhere else.

I look down the road and see a commotion. Word is out that the cops are on the street. True to rumour, three plainclothes pigs appear. One has a photograph in his hand and they show the picture to anyone who bothers to stick around to look. Most of the people, vendors, hookers and dealers, turn and slither away, disappear. Cops are never good news here.

I draw nearer. They show a passport-sized picture of a blonde white girl, maybe 15 or 16 years old. She's missing. 'Has anyone seen her?' they ask. Everyone shakes their heads. No-one knows, no-one knows a thing round here.

Two days later her body's found chopped up in a big municipal dustbin in an alleyway round the corner behind the garage on Soper Road. It's been rotting for weeks. No-one knew her and no-one's missed her. Story comes out that she got into a car with two white men, two weeks back. They gave her R300 to buy crack and screw her. She was away for a while; then, when she returned, she gave them something through the window and ran off. Their 'rocks' were six small pebbles. They didn't take too kindly to being ripped off. They searched for her the whole night and when they found her, they took her to a quiet snaky alleyway. There they showed the fucking little whore who was the boss.

This tragic tale falls on deaf ears. I carry on knocking men. There's no lesson for me or anyone here in the story. Life is cheap, death and life interchange, there is no real difference in this ghetto.

The 'steamers', as these men are sometimes referred to, are often addicted to both sex and drugs and they are easy targets. I get a weird kick, a power surge knocking them. I find the only semblance of any power I have left in taking money off these pricks, promising them all sorts of things and then disappearing with their cash to smoke as many rocks as I can.

It's easy to con these desperados who snake and snail past the hookers looking for some kind of release, something to fill the holes in their souls. It seems that the streets are our age's new churches. The redemption the sex worshippers seek is momentarily found in some whore's mouth, that wafer biscuit they crave in a crack pipe. The forgetting, the mission, the escape, the union with what seems like an Almighty is found for a moment in a hooker's heartless hands.

––––––––––––

It's 1984 ... that Inspector of Religion asks: *'Who made the chair? Who made the trees? The wood? How did it all begin? Who started it all?'*

Back then I couldn't really say for sure. Now I stand before him, my eyes are black holes, my pupils stare straight ahead, they drill right through him.

'In the beginning was the Word, and the Word was Crack ... and on the seventh day there was no rest. Crack said: "I Am that I Am. I am a jealous God, and you shall have no gods before Me ... Go forth and multiply the rocks ye shall smoke. Find any ways and means to fill that hole in your soul."'

And I did.

––––––––––––

I'd always wondered why throughout history men had found the need to seek out prostitutes to satisfy a sexual urge. I had in the past been slightly threatened by these women who were able to do a transaction, perform a sexual favour, get paid and move on. No emotional tugging at the heart strings, no possession and control issues. Just wham, in, out, up, down, whatever – and move on.

There are women out there, 'normal' women who wouldn't dream of being hookers, who look down at whores, but whose husbands or partners visit them regularly and treat their wives at home much worse. These women have to put up with untold abuse and demands and at the end of the day they have sold their pussies for a washing machine or, if they are lucky, a tumble dryer. Then one wonders who, in fact, is getting exploited and abused? And who is the real whore here?

―――――――――

My lungs are bleeding when I hack cough; I haven't slept for over a week now. I hardly eat. I can't stop talking – it's like a string of close to psychotic ramblings pour out of me. Perhaps the train of traumas unaddressed, first the boys being ripped away from me and everything that followed – the rape, the beatings, the tricks and all the rest – have piled up. Then, of course, to top it all, the overload of cocaine has just proved too much for my system.

But go home? It's the last thing I think of. I have no home. *This* is my home. My lives run out, and then – like those of a very naughty cloning cat – they recreate themselves: I have used far more than nine … My family, friends, all escape routes from the 'Brow, have become remote and distant impossibilities.

CHAPTER 23

OVER AND OUT

It's 3 am on a Monday night, the La Rosa Hotel, and I'm sitting in the foyer lounge. Outside the wind screams icy. July 1999, the winter before the millennium and it's the coldest in years. My bony knees scream blue in the dead night chill. I watch the few die-hards outside. Skirts thigh-high, hitched up, begging for a car to stop and show them some cash. I look for a victim inside – it's slightly warmer here. Then the front door swings open – my eyes latch onto the new arrival.

He's a black cowboy-like dude. Piff Daddy. He's got gold bling bling. His red Beamer, no number plates, is parked outside and he's one angry motherfucker come in from the cold on some dark mission. He's deep in an animated rap talk to the security guy at reception. I edge in closer to get the buzz.

'There's this white bitch, she's in here somewhere. I need to find her. She says her name's Fatima. I gave her cash and now I been waiting for more than an hour for this bitch to come back. She's about this high, white girl, dark hair like ... *that* one (he points at me). I paid good money for white pussy. Now what you gonna do about it? I need some help.'

The security stares at him, blank face, he doesn't give a fuck.

Fatima has been particularly revolting to me since my arrival. I know where her room is. I get an idea. 'I know where she is,' I sidle up to him, pimp serpentine sell-out. 'You want some help. How much do you think it's worth?'

Oh, gosh, how clever I've become, I'm really getting good at this, I smile to myself.

He shows me a wad of 100s. He's got a silver Magnum strapped across his chest. 'I'll give one grando if you deliver her to me. COD.'

———————

'Suck my cock.'

He's undoing his belt and trying to push hard against me in the lift as we shudder up to the 12th floor.

'Hang on, I'm trying to take you to Fatima – then *she* can do what you paid her for. Just wait a second, now.'

I squirm out of his pushy groin and brandy breath. Then, just in time, the lift stops on the 12th.

In front of Room 1207 I knock and call her name. Loud music is blaring from inside. *'Celebrate good times, c'mon.'* Sounds like there's a party going on inside there on El Gangsta's cash. I bang and bang, louder and louder, my voice blaring down the empty corridor. She's in there, that's for sure, but no-one's saying they're home.

'So, well, here's her room. I have done my part of the deal – can I get my cash now?'

He turns on me like some vicious python, grabs me, spits in my face and pushes me onto my knees, holding my head as he undoes his belt.

'Suck me, you fucking bitch! Now give me what I paid for!!'

Somehow I manage to squirm-crawl away. The lift is still waiting there on the 12th floor. I manage to leap in and close it, just as he gets there. I push the ground floor button, my heart screaming, beating to get out.

I rush into the foyer; it's empty besides the security guard who's sleeping open-mouthed at his desk. Next thing El Gangsta is behind me. He's caught the other lift. He's got me from behind; I feel the cold thud of metal on the side of my face. He's got his gun to my head. The security sleeps on.

His grip bruises my fleshless arm. Time has slowed down. It feels like everything has come to this, to this aching moment, long it stretches, like elastic distended. Oh God, *now* I am going to die and no-one will ever know me! The gun rests long and slow. Then I hear a click. I wait. Nothing. I hear another. Nothing. Then a loud shot rings, blacks out the night, and glass splits apart. The front window screams into sharded shatters. He lets go of me. He leaves, Black Highwayman. I stay frozen to the spot.

I got shot and I'm not dead, I hear it over and over again in my head. I got shot. I'm not dead.

I find a man who buys me rocks. I smoke into the night.

It's 10 am. I have not slept. I'm cruising the foyer. I'm taken from behind by Fatima. She catches me off balance – that's not hard – I'm skinny and all over the place, rocked up to my eyeballs. I feel a sharp stiletto rip into my lip. 'Fucking bitch! It's time for you to die!' she screams into my face. I grab an empty beer bottle lying against a ledge. She kicks it out of my hand. I'm on the floor now. I crawl to the door. I'm out in the bright morning cutting air. The sun screams into my eyes.

I fall. I stumble -

- and I come face to face with my brother and sister. I hardly see them. They see me. They have come to look for me and appear like two angels, at the exact moment when I perhaps need them most. But I can't take the blinding light right now. I run. I have come so far, I have to escape. I'm bulldozed by everything that made me ache, that I left behind. They remind me of the pain, of what once was and right now, I want none of it.

I'm running across Abel Road, where to I don't know, but I want to leave them all behind and keep moving, keep moving. A car bashes into the side of me, my thigh blotches black bruise. I run to the hotel round the corner, the one I came to six weeks back. I want drugs. I don't want to be found and taken away from this. I have come too far. Gone to down. Fucked up too much, I can't go back.

Then they are there behind me, my brother in his shiny Beamer and my sister next to him.

I hide behind the barbed wire in the parking lot next to a bin. They're there on top of me, grabbing and pulling me. *'Nooooo-o-o-o-oooooooo, fuck off, you Nazis! Noo-o-oo!!!!'*

My shrieking cracked-out voice cuts the air like piano wire. Goodluck appears from nowhere. He opens the door, he picks me up, he puts me in, the car door locks, damn central locking. They drive me away. Yazmean screams, I scream and the beasty voice screams loudest of all: *'NOO-O-O-OO!!!'*

PART 3

RECOVERY

CHAPTER 24

ENOCH'S WALK: THE ROBOT PEOPLE

I'm toiling on a farm amongst a group of leather hard destitutes. Alkies, hardened druggies, outies, jailbirds, the robot people are my companions in a dirt ditch – and I, once queen of my own orchestrated reality, goddess of my own dreams and schemes, am digging in a red earth trench alongside the rubbish dump brigade, society's throw-aways. Under the hood of the azure African sky we move in time, shovelling sand, chopping rock. Dolomite.

I'm digging for my life, rock for rock, boulder for boulder – deeper and deeper, I dig. My tears form rivers down my soil-streaked cheeks. Regrets. Where is my full-time maid now, where are my two baby sons, my flesh, my blood that I have swopped for a rock, a little bag of brown, of smack? I'm smacked big time out of the veneer of my northern suburb heritage, my drama school accent, my larney words, my knowledge, my trivia – all useless now.

Hours seems like years. Minutes are centuries. The sweat beats out of me. I trip. I stumble. I fall. I'm brought to my knees. Now it's just me and God's landscape. *'For everything there is a season and a time for every purpose under the heavens.'* Ecclesiastes – Sunday school verses bunch in on me.

I cannot help but get real now. I am forced into the here and now. I am free, a slave, a prisoner all at once. I am part of some derelict destitute dance … in the queue of the homeless soup line-up and now I am forced to consider how I got here. How I landed on a rubbish heap of life, penniless, prospectless, homeless and meaningless. I am forced to search myself with an aching truth comb – it makes me throb and sob. And every illusion I ever had fades away.

After my siblings pull me out of Hillbrow, I am taken to my sister's home. No-one wants to look at me, let alone touch me. I am wearing a tiny, tiny white mini-dress that barely covers my ass, torn black stockings and a pair of scuffed stilettos I have picked up somewhere on my travels. My sister runs me a bath and I think she throws bleach or some type of detergent in it, as it seems to burn through my paper-thin skin. My mother has been summoned and she can only shake her head when she looks at me and say: 'Oh, my darling – look how thin you are!'

My sister takes the strong arm approach and orders me around like a Fraülein Himmler on a bad acid trip. In the bath I feel each vertebra in my spine bruising into the hard enamel. I have lost so much weight on my crack-and-nothing-else diet that my hip bones jut out like a famine-struck Ethiopian's.

My sister bashes into the bathroom without knocking. 'Hurry up and get dressed! Someone called David is going to take you to a place in the Magaliesberg. It's a rehab of sorts because *we* can't look after you and you obviously need help.'

'Who the fuck is David? I'm not going anywhere. You can't make me!' I try to push my head under the water.

'I'm giving you 10 minutes in here,' she barks. 'Hurry up and get dressed!'

———————————

'I just want to share a meal with my mother.' I'm out the bath now and dressed in my white mini and my mother's cream jersey. I insist on wearing it.

I plead with my sister. 'Please. I haven't eaten something for so long and I want to eat with Mommy.'

'Let her, let her share a meal with me,' my mother supports my case.

'She's just trying to play for time. It's the drugs talking, not her.' My sister matter-of-factly throws a piece of toast my way and begins looking for her car keys. She has made arrangements to drop me at some dickhead called David who will take me to a place called Enoch's Walk. I have heard her making arrangements for my life while I've been bathing.

But I am one step ahead; I have found her car keys and hidden them carefully between the pillows on the sofa. No-one is going find them there …

At no point do I see what a desperately bad state I am in, how awful and haggard and cracked up and crazy I am. From my viewpoint I am fine, great, in control, and everyone *else* is screwed up and cruel. I am caught in a typical junkie blaming victim mode circle. 'You don't have to waste your time looking for your keys. I have swallowed them!' I say to my sister triumphantly.

She is not sure whether I am kidding or not. No-one can tell where my head is at. Nothing is really beyond the realms of possibilities with me right now.

'I've swallowed them, so don't even bother trying to send me anywhere. I am a human being, you know, and I do have my rights.'

For the next 30 minutes I watch my family and sister's housemate search for the keys. I grin. She grabs my arm and it feels like it is bruising right through.

'Tell me where the keys are!' She slaps me really hard.

'You fucking Nazi! Why don't you just let me eat with my mother? That is all I wanted to do. Why do you have to treat me like I am some kind of terrible animal?'

'Because you *are* – you are despicable!' she screams at me.

In the interim David has arrived to take me away, as my sister has informed him of the key story. 'NOO-O-O-OOOO!' I scream as I'm drop-kicked and loaded into the old Merc that waits ominously to ferry me away. *'NOO-O-O-OOO!'* my beasty addict voice screams louder and shrivels up a little in the cold, dank, blaring noontime light.

―――――

So I'm dumped unceremoniously on a farm in the Magaliesberg called Enoch's Walk. It was started years back by a Christian preacher who wanted to offer the homeless a chance to pull themselves together and work on the farm in exchange for food and shelter. The surroundings are beautiful, the farm nestled in the Waterberg and near Bobbejaanskloof.

It is near the place where one of SA's most talented writers, Eugene Marais, most famous for his book, *The Soul of the White Ant*, spent much of his time. Like me, he was a morphine/heroin addict. Legend has it that one night he had run out of his gear. It was raining really hard and no-one would drive through to Pretoria to get him his fix. At about 2 am he made his way through the terrible storming conditions to the neighbouring farm, where he asked to borrow a gun to shoot a troublesome snake. Minutes later the neighbour heard two shots and Marais, one of our finest minds, was dead.

I feel somehow better knowing that another like me had spent time near to where I now found myself, lost and alone.

When I trip-fall onto the homeless farm, I must surely be a sight to behold. Old men, bent arthritic, crooked and swollen-purple-handed from too many winters on park benches, mill around. I see a man, deformed ears and definite incest lineage, sipping cooldrink from a bowl. When I am offered a similar vessel to drink from, I howl: 'I'm not a fucking dog – I am not drinking out of that! Give me a cup! I am not a dog!'

In fact, I was far below any dog – I was impossible, ungrateful, unkind, vicious, withdrawing from huge amounts of drugs, traumatised and raving.

No-one really quite knows what to do with me. People here pray a lot and it seems the only thing to do with this mad, screeching witch is to ask the good Lord to cleanse her and save her soiled soul.

'Will Jesus love me if I tell you that I am a Muslim?' I have taken 'Yazmean's' red silk scarf out of the 'Brow and wear it now, on the second day, to early morning prayers.

'I am a Muslim – will my soul be saved?' I shout from the back in the little stone makeshift church.

There is an awkward silence. I have disturbed the order of things. Someone giggles. No-one knows how to answer my ranting question.

'No,' announces the pastor finally, knowing he is probably about to be set up. 'No – being a Muslim is unacceptable. Unfortunately, the Scriptures say only through the blood of Jesus will you be saved.'

'Bullshit!' I shout. 'That is bullshit! I don't think God said that. *You* say that. Actually, how do *any* of you know what God is saying? Have you spoken to Him on your phone lately? What's He on – MTN or Vodacom?'

There is a hollow, embarrassed silence. Then the pastor clears his podgy throat and announces that we shall now sing *Amazing Grace*. Everyone sings especially loudly when they get to: '… *That saved a wretch like me, I once was lost but now I'm found, was blind but now I see …*' and look really hard at me, as though trying to throw some good sense to my lost and blasphemous soul.

———

The problem with withdrawing from crack is not a physical one like heroin, where you shake and crawl and writhe in agony: instead, a totally disturbed and shattered psyche emerges. Over the next week, sleep evades me as if I am undergoing sleep deprivation torture in some remote Vietcong camp. When everyone else is in dreamland, I roam the camp's gardens. I find myself at 2 am looking for Jesus, wanting to have an argument with Him about why He doesn't dig Muslims. I look for an angel, anyone to share a chat with. I am not well.

After a week no-one can handle my ravings and babblings and I am taken to a clinic in the nearby suburb of Laudeum, the area designated to the Indian population after they were forcibly removed from Sophiatown years back in the days of apartheid.

The problem begins when I am dropped outside the clinic and left alone while the three men driving the farm truck move on to pick up supplies and do the farm's daily business. I decide to go into the clinic, have an HIV test and ask them for sleeping pills. They do the HI test. Although the window period is too short, I know that it will be negative because in all the time I spent in Hillbrow – even during my rape – the use of condoms was *de rigeur*. It was incredible how in the middle of the city's highest risk and hottest sex spot, it seemed to be the safest-sex, most condom-conscious spot in the land. As far as sleeping pills go, they tell me to go to a GP.

It's 10 am, my business at the clinic is over and now I have nothing to do – and me being left to my own devices in my present state of mind is highly inadvisable.

I decide I need a drink. I find a shebeen, but I have no cash and cajole and beg the man for a quart of Black Label. I sit next to a bush for shade, down the beer. Within minutes I fall asleep. I wake with a splitting headache in the midday sun, disorientated and unsure of where the hell I am.

I decide I need to find some crack, but realise the possibilities are highly unlikely, not knowing anyone or anything in this place. I know finding a joint or some dagga will be far easier and so I set off on a scoring mission. No-one seems to know anything here. They are probably completely suspicious of this white woman who seems a bit crazy, asking them questions like: 'Where can I get dope?' They probably think I am some kind of informer.

I finally flag down an Afrikaner-looking man with the requisite moustache who is driving a white car.

'Uh, do you think you can help me?' I sidle over. 'I really, really need something to smoke. Do you know where I can get some dagga?'

'Sure,' he says, opening the passenger side to let me in. 'I know where you can get plenty of dagga. Only one problem, though – I'm a cop.'

A cop? I don't flinch, moving seamlessly into second gear.

'Great. Then you will definitely know where I can get some. I'm sure you have a lot in your confiscated stash.' He stares at me.

'You can't give me some crack, by any chance, can you?'

He laughs out loud and shakes his head.

'No, I'm sorry. I can't, but let me take you somewhere – maybe I can organise a bit of dagga on the side for you.'

'I don't have any cash, but I will pay you back some day,' I lie.

'It's fine,' he says. 'No worries.'

On the way I begin to tell him some of my sorry tale. He hangs onto every word and it seems he knows the farm I'm staying on pretty well.

He does organise for me, a nice little fistful of good stuff and he drops me back at the clinic. Much to my surprise, a few weeks later he comes to visit me at Enoch's Walk. Maybe he was a bit intrigued by me, the washed-out crazy junkie, maybe he liked my knees, who knows – but I must say, for a change I was impressed with the prompt and dedicated service of the SAPS.

––––––––––

For days and nights I carry on not sleeping. My mind is unhinged and working at speeds unheard of. On and on – over and over it works and my mouth follows suit, religiously. I smoke all the cop's dope and then – good little druggy that I am – I find a source on the farm and begin swopping all my supplies like washing powder, sugar and coffee for little matchboxes of dope. The prospect of being completely clean has not even dawned on me yet. I am still in deep denial addict mode. But I guess an important step in the bigger picture has been taken. I am out of Hillbrow and I am not smoking heroin or crack. Smoking dagga for me seemed to be a way to make that transition.

I'm finally taken to a 'proper' doctor who makes a somewhat inaccurate diagnosis of me, prescribing me Ritalin to prevent post-cocaine depression. But I am manic – not depressed – and the medication makes me even worse, more hyper than ever. So for yet another week, sleep evades me.

I hardly notice the inmates on the homeless farm in my first fortnight there. But, like rehab back in '96, the cast list comprises a fistful of fascinating human specimens. First there's:

Buddy: Buddy in a torn and holey green jersey, Buddy of the purple-hand brigade who had permanent eczema and frostbite on his plump, swollen fingers spent on so many park benches that he could have got timeshare around the country in parks … he is a miserable, embittered soul who hates everybody. All he ever says to me is: 'You remind me of a girl I once met in a bar. I bought her a drink. It soon turned out to be much more than one. I thought she would go home with me, but at the end of the night she said "fuck you". Well, fuck *you*, I say.' And he spits at me and shuffles off on his bunion onion feet, towards the flowerbed that he's spent the last year weeding. Buddy has been coming to the farm every winter for over a decade. As soon as summer comes he will be back in the city parks, alcohol-soaked until the winter's frosty breath chases him back to the Walk.

Then there is **Dimitri,** a sexy Greek who's been a heroin addict since the late '80s. He lived in Hillbrow in the '90s and has now given his heart and soul to the Lord and is working like a pack-horse on the farm and learning the Old Testament verbatim. He's brought along his hooker girlfriend, Macy, who he used to pimp in the 'Brow and – true to his junkie control freak nature – he's mending her ways, getting her Bible-bashed so he can marry her in the spring and live happily ever after on the farm. (Seems the plan did not quite work out – he got drunk one night and took a duck off the farm. I saw him two years ago, skeletal, trampy and homeless, begging at a robot near the 'Brow. Macy was nowhere to be seen …)

There is **Betsy Boswagter,** a tiny little Afrikaans woman who lives in a caravan on the farm and every morning goes twig and wood hunting. Her face is wrinkled brown leather, a testament to the harsh African climatic conditions. She has spent much of her life in orphanages and at robots begging for money. She seems as happy as a pig in shit on the farm and stashes everything she comes across in her caravan, under her bed and in boxes that, like her dreams, are piled to the ceiling.

Pastor Steven is a podgy dodgy dude with an even podgier pig trotter-like wife called **Beryl** … Pastor Steven has a very wandering set of peepers – on numerous occasions I catch him leching on my fishnetted leg or on any other woman who vaguely shows an inch of flesh. His fire-and-brimstone services are designed to keep the homeless in fear and instil in them a terrible sense of foreboding if they ever leave the farm … I very soon decide there is a direct intent to keep us all as weak and frightened as possible to ensure a constant supply of devotees and free labour for the farm. For although we receive meals free of charge, they are all donated from a supermarket and long past their expiry date. What better way to keep a farm going without cost and throw dog bones at the people daily? Most cults across the globe operate on a similar basis.

Andréa walks around with a hood on her head, her bright blue eyes peeping modestly out, framed by a halo of golden hair. She likes to tell us she is the bride of Jesus … Andréa is a beautiful girl who was pulled off the streets of Hillbrow by the Bible-bashers after sucking too much dick for crack. On some days she is covered and demure, then on others her street side reappears and her swagger and cursing begin. (She ran away three times while I was there … the last time no-one could find her. Today she may be dead, or in a nunnery – who knows?)

Simon is the scarecrow-thin owner of the Walk, which he inherited from his pastor dad. He is 36 years old, unmarried and constantly in search of a wife. Each night he prays at his bedside for God to send him the virgin Christian girl of his dreams. His judgement is often clouded when it comes to matters of the skirt. (I twisted him every which way around my finger, but it was largely through his good graces and kindness of heart that I was able to leave the Walk once I finally did get clean and set on a path forward.)

But by far the most seductive presence, interspersed in this crowd of crazy people ... a shining light appears to me in the form of ... **Donovan.**

It's day 15 of sleeplessness. I have found a makeshift gym in a rusty caravan trailer and am pumping iron every day, running on a very basic makeshift treadmill, trying to rid myself of some of my manic energy when I suddenly sense the presence of someone in the dark corner. At first I am not sure if it's a man or woman, as the person in the shadows has long, beautiful Raphaelite locks and is slender. On closer inspection, I can see it's a he.

His name is Donovan; he lives in a cottage on the farm. His brother shares it with him. He's an artist – his mother works in the art department in the movies and she lives in another house further along the red dirt road. Donovan is an artist! That makes me so happy. I have found a kindred spirit here in the middle of nowhere!

I immediately see his hands are paint-speckled. He is one of the most beautiful people I have seen in a very long time. He looks like a lean, gorgeous angel and, to be sure, the gifts he gives me over the next few weeks are truly of angelic quality.

He teaches me how to draw, to paint, to see things out of my head, to put down objectives. Donovan in many ways becomes as close to a human saviour as is possible. I project everything onto him. I tell him my story over and over again. In his patient, very quiet and observant way, he listens to each word I utter and once in a while he says something really slowly and gently which gives me the strength and incentive to move on. He is wide open for my pain – he takes it on, he is old, he is ancient, he is wise. He is 27 years old and he becomes my friend.

I want to crawl right into him, get lost and get him to fix me up and let me forget, forget. We meet every day in the gym and then we move on to the crafts room, where we create things all day. We share poems with each other. He shows me his art. I think he's brilliant and he thinks the same of me. A mutual admiration club can do wonders for the tattered soul.

Somewhere between the sessions in the gym and the hours spent bent over paintings and poems, we begin to have an illicit affair. It's illicit for there are, of course, countless rules on the homeless camp preventing the inmates from getting dirty with each other. The fact that Donovan is not part of the Walk but lives on the property would make the situation even worse if anyone were to find out about it. Our relationship is sweet and very therapeutic. None of the abuse or crazy stuff I was exposed to in Hillbrow. This is slow and shy and gentle. I fall head over heels. People start to notice that we are spending a lot of time with each other. People will often try to break things apart, especially when they are reborn Christians who believe the flesh is evil and sex is sinful.

I don't care. I ignore them. Then we are banned from seeing each other – I don't care, we ignore them and meet in late moonlight gardens at the edge of the farm river. I draw my first drawing, paint my first work. I find bits of enamel, plaka paint, a 1 m x 0.5 m piece of interesting wood on a rubbish dump – and my first painting emerges, which I call *The She-Devil and the Blank Girl*. A Modesty Blaze-type, naked, black-haired, comic strip-like woman holds a faceless hooker in fishnets as if controlling her. In the background a window reveals the Hillbrow cityscape.

I begin to make clay vases, working, working with my hands – it keeps my tongue still. I have finally started sleeping.

CHAPTER 25

LAZARUS BABE

I adopt a little piggy. I call her Babe. Of course, she reminds me of that little piggy from the film. It was always my son Joy's favourite movie. She is on her last breath, only a couple of days old and about to be thrown to her death in the farm river when I am overwhelmed by a maternal urge, and rescue her. I grab her to my breast, wrap the semi-conscious little creature up in a woollen blanket and begin feeding her water through a dropper. She is dehydrated and hardly breathing. Day and night I hold vigil with the piggy, praying and willing life back into her. If I could inject my breath into her mouth and give her artificial resuscitation, I would. It seems like the most important thing I have ever done in my life – trying to keep this little pink, helpless thing alive.

As I hold her and try to keep her warm, it is my own raw, red, barely pumping, crack-sodden heart that I am stroking, massaging, and willing back to life. She is me. I am her … sad, broken little baby.

My good friend Kaz comes to visit me on the red earth farm with her crippled baby baboon, Darwin, in tow. I am not to this day sure how she hears that I am on the farm, but she is one of my only old-life connections with whom I have not messed up irreparably. She lives on a farm nearby in the Bobbejaanskloof and is trying to rehabilitate Darwin into a troop of wild baboons. She adopted him when he was just a few weeks old after a farmer shot his mother, who was carrying him. The weight of her dead body crippled him.

She takes one look at Babe and offers to take her to a vet nearby. Two days later piggy is brought back, a brand-new Babe! She has been put on drips and fed glucose, she has pulled through and has now taken a dramatic turn for the better. Kaz brings me newborn human baby's nappies and a baby's bottle and I throw myself full force into becoming a mother to a little pig.

Soon Babe is on her feet and shadowing me wherever I go. People get used to the sight of me with my pig in tow. She sleeps beside me in my bed at night and during the compulsory church sessions she squeals and squeaks during the prayers, which always gives me a much-needed excuse to escape. Maybe she's a Muslim piggy 'cos she doesn't seem to like those long, boring services …

Soon she is growing beyond all predictions and by the end of the second month, she is tearing my room to pieces and making a God Almighty mess – but I love her and I sense I am replacing all my truncated and cut-off feelings for my two sons onto this pink and squealy funny creature, who thinks she is a dog.

Babe is an angel who makes me believe that perhaps I *can* take care of something, and that I am not all bad and not a complete failure. She gets me out of the loops of self-obsession that sometimes bury me into coma-like compulsion.

People – or, rather, this stupid flock of human sheep – become resentful that I get special treatment, that I am allowed to wander around the farm looking after a silly pig and paint with Donovan, basically doing my own thing, while everyone else is forced to do hard labour for their bread. Meetings are called behind my back by some of the inmates and plans to curb my errant ways are discussed in harsh, urgent whispers.

Finally I'm called in front of the committee, the pedantic Politburo, I call them. I am told I have to do more 'serious labour', that I am messing around and not pulling my weight. I make a suggestion. On the far side of the property a huge metal blackened-out structure stands. It caught my eye on the first day I arrived, a month back. It is the foundation and structure of a church that burnt down a couple of years back.

I come up with a way out and – I guess – a completely impractical plan. I propose to de-rust the structure, sand it down and make a church for the farm. It will be made completely out of stained glass; I can see it clearly in my mind's eye as I describe it in rapturous tones to the Politburo, who glare at me from moustachioed leather faces. No-one says a word. Probably because they are staring open-mouthed at me, not believing what a crazy idea has just come out of mine.

Simon, the owner of the farm, is completely taken with me, and his word is final authority. He likes my idea and throws his support behind me. So each morning I don overalls, go to my work station, light a fat joint, put piggy next to me and start derusting and scraping the metal. It keeps me occupied for hours on end. At the end of the day I meet Donovan and paint or write and later we play Scrabble at his mother's house and then disappear for a secret liaison in the moonlight at the river. Slowly my life seems to be taking on a pretty pleasant turn. I have put on some weight, my muscles are growing. I'm almost halfway normal!

One day I receive a phone call. I don't recognise the voice at first, then I realise it's Boy 2, my husband! I had all but forgotten about him. He is out of rehab now and he wants to bring Joy to visit me. I am shocked and stunned and terrified all at once. So much has happened in the last two months... how will it be to see him again, he who was once central to my life? So much to explain, so much distance between us...

He would like to come the following day. My heart is beating really fast when I put down the phone. Oh, God, what shall I wear? I have come to the Walk with no wardrobe, as I have lost all my belongings on my travels and I now have only a few donated dresses from a charitable church – hardly what I would call 'nice clothes'. Ah, well, he's a motherfucker anyway – why even make the effort?

Nevertheless, the following day I comb my hair and try to look my best. I watch the clock snail along until it's the time of their expected arrival.

Boy 2 looks different, fatter, cleaner, older, I forget how grey his hair is, when he walks down the garden to meet me. My son has grown – I haven't seen him in about four months. I hug him. He squirms away, sees Babe the pig and begins chasing and playing with her. I'm relieved, it gets me off the uncomfortable hook of what to do with my visitors. I feel so awkward. Joy chases Babe all over the garden.

Boy 2 has come with his friend, Darryl, who was once my shoe-stealing accomplice back in 1996. He's also cleaned up. It feels as if Boy 2 is embarrassed and almost afraid of me. There is so much to tell him, yet I can't find the words, any words to say anything meaningful at all. Instead I ramble on about the church that I am 'building'.

'Come, let me show you,' I pull my visitors with me and proudly climb up the structure. They watch me from below.

'I am giving myself two years to rebuild this church. I am going to cover it in stained glass and then I am going to live here forever. I am going to get so high! I will be a human messenger for God,' I tell them triumphantly from the area I have designated for the steeple. I probably act more crazily on purpose so Boy 2 will leave the farm, worried and perplexed about the state of his 'wife'.

I catch Boy 2 glancing at Darryl, frowning and biting his lip. He thinks I am insane. I know it. I can feel that's what he's thinking. Maybe I am, I am. I want them to go now.

Now I don't like this feeling.

I have hardly spent a moment with my son. I don't know what to do with him. I realise that I am really not the same person I used to be. But then, I guess I *never* really knew what to do with him. I don't know who I am anymore. I want a joint now. They must leave. As we walk to the car, Boy 2 stops and says:

'I have met another woman. Her name is Marie. She is two years clean and she has children almost the same age as ours, a bit older. I am going be moving in with her soon. I thought I had better tell you.' He does not look at me.

'Is she the one who was sitting next to you at that meeting I came to?'

He nods.

'That's nice,' I say. I am hardly listening to him. I want them to leave. Now.

———————

I hardly give him a second thought, I carry on with my life on the farm, sanding that metal church, smoking my joints and playing with Donovan. The pain of having to imbibe everything Boy 2 represented and incited in me would be far too hard to bear right now, so I retreat into Lala land. Then, once again, just as I think I have everything in order and that it's all going my way, something happens that changes it all.

———————

I am caught by Donovan's mother in a compromising position, half-naked with her son on the floor of his cottage one Sunday when we think everyone's in church. She flips out and runs to Simon and the pastor, and spews a diatribe of hatred against the 'drug addict whore' who has come to devour her boy. 'Jezebel from hell' is what she calls me. It reminds me of my mother-in-law's last dialogue.

As my luck would have it, I have also just been bust the day before for smoking joints. Now I see how I sabotaged my situation completely. At the time, however, I simply believed I was being victimised by dumb sheep. The two combined transgressions warrant my expulsion.

'We are sorry, but you were warned. You were aware of the rules when you arrived and now you must leave,' says Simon, the great Lord overseer. He feels torn, but pressure by the Politburo is forcing him to act this way.

'Oh, please,' I beg. 'I have nowhere to go, please don't throw me out!'

But they are unrelenting. It is a committee decision. I am expelled.

As I pack my few belongings into a plastic packet, I think: How can a person be thrown off a homeless farm? That must be almost the most difficult thing to happen to anyone.

As I drag myself out of the door, I hear the lilting tone of Bob Dylan singing crackly on the pastor's portable radio. It feels as if he wrote that song just for me. '*Once upon a time you looked so fine, beautiful in your prime, now didn't you? People called to say "beware", they were only kidding you … You used to talk about everybody that was hanging out, now you don't talk so loud, now you don't seem so proud about having to be scrounging for your last meal ... So how does it feel to be all alone, with no direction home, a complete unknown, like a rolling stone? ... '*

They agree not to tell my mother the reasons for my having to leave. They call her and tell her they think I need to come home the next day.

This time round my mother is not very happy to see me. She and her husband lead a peaceful, uneventful life, they watch birds in the garden and start drinking at 4 pm. They are happy in their cocoon. I am a disturbed and unruly presence who breaks their routine. But I am my mother's daughter, her flesh and blood, and I know she knows I have nowhere else to go.

The room I am given in her home has a cupboard filled to the seams with alcohol. It freaks me out completely – all that drink and I can't touch it! By the end of the fifth day home, I phone Simon on the Walk and beg and plead to return. 'Jesus forgave the sinners, why can't you?' I weep, manipulatively. I paint a picture of my situation in such a dire and awful light that his heart melts. He tells me I may have one more chance.

So I pack my things together, wave goodbye once again to my relieved mother and go back to the farm.

On arriving, I head straight for the pig section and look for Babe. I call her and whistle and oink. It smells dreadful at the bottom at the pens. There are over 100 pigs rolling around in mud and swill and my Babe, who grew so big before I left, could be anywhere. I race back up to the house and bang on Simon's door.

'I've just been down to the pigs and I wanted to say hello to Babe, but I can't find her,' I gasp breathless. 'Can you come down with me and show me where she is?'

Simon looks awkward and turns a bright shade of red.

'Uh, I'm not sure how to tell you this ... two days ago Babe was put on the truck and taken to the pig auction. By now she's probably bacon.'

Babe is dead. Oh no!

The killing of Babe cuts me deep, slashes my newborn soul. It is as though someone has butchered the smallest, most tender part of me, the part that has only just begun to learn to trust again. It is as though they have killed me too.

I am four years old – my Daddy is dead. Everything elongates around me. I am growing smaller and smaller by the minute, little mad sad Alice ...

Within an hour of learning of the cruel ending to my Babe, all my resolve to behave myself evaporates. I score a matchbox of dope from a farm labourer and smoke a joint, stashing half of it on the concrete windowsill. I want to get lost, displace the sorrow that engulfs and throttles me.

The maid has been watching me and she is dying to have me expelled as she thinks I have come back to marry her master Simon. Oh, my God! I have been back there for just an hour and I am expelled again. Kicked off the homeless farm for the second time! And if I ever had a lightbulb moment, this was it. It was time to change. Everything.

This time I go down on my knees and plead and beg the homeless committee. I know I really do not have anywhere to go, except Hillbrow, and I really can't go back there. They finally agree to let me stay and place me under very strict conditions. I am given a drug urine test, which of course tests positive for THC, the chemical found in dagga. It usually takes a long time – at least a month – to clear out a user's system. For the first time since I have been on the Walk, I agree to abide by all the rules and be a good girl.

So on 1 September 1999, I celebrate my first real day clean and sober.

It is as though someone has sandpapered all my skin off me and – just like piggy Babe was once small and pink and raw – I now face my world defenceless, burnt by reality. Hours seem like years, centuries. Time – when last did I keep track of time?

Like the little mermaid who was granted her wish for feet in exchange for her tail, each step I take feels as if I am walking on mountains of glass. Not since I was 11 years old have I not used a drink or a drug to displace my feelings …

that's 22 years of living in a progressive, dimming coma. The ladder of life looms sky-high – monstrous before me.

I now start the very daunting uphill climb of my real recovery. I've been on it ever since.

Without anything to blur or numb the reality of my life, I begin to see things clearly for the first time in years.

I am fucked. Well and truly fucked. I have caused untold pain in people's lives and I have messed up all my chances and everything good that was ever given to me. I have taken myself to the brink of self-destruction and now I am empty and absolutely devastated by this new-found awareness.

Perhaps this is my first real spiritual awakening – it says very loudly and very clearly: 'The party is over! The party is over, and you have overstayed your welcome by years. Now it's time to start fixing it up.' But where to begin? Where to begin on this roofless self?

The traumatic after-shocks have created a huge hole, a vacuum in me and as each day passes on the homeless farm, I realise I am hiding away from real life and the real responsibilities that I need to confront. My children have been reunited with their father, I have a baby whom I haven't seen in months and a toddler – the pain begins to penetrate me.

On the 54th day of being clean, I test negative for any drugs in my system. Within days I announce that I have decided to leave the farm. Armed with my urine test, I feel as if it is now or never that I make the break. I am terrified to go back, but I know I have to. I call my mother, explain my decision and ask her if I can come home. After a long pause, she sighs long-sufferingly and hardly audibly mutters: 'OK.'

CHAPTER 26

THE REMOTE OF HOME

I sit in my mother's house on the bed I was conceived on. My mother's house, the cradle of my addictions. The hum of the fridge is my sad lullaby.

The phone is locked. They don't trust me here. Don't blame them. Too many dealers to be reached through Telkom's crackly lines. There is no ringing for me, no husband, no lover, no friend to take me away from it all. It's 10 am, I will myself back to sleep, perchance to dream. There is nothing much else to do.

Later, I awake sweaty. An anaesthetic clod clouds my head. Dwarf baby I stumble out of bed. It's 11.30 am; I am beckoned to the fridge. I open it, am blinded by the light. Food, once an old pill of pleasure, holds no appeal. I close it quickly.

I move past the bar in my mother's home. Glinting bottles filled and lined up in alcoholic promises, they wink at me, do little hip wiggles, beckon and call to me. I close my hand that would like to reach out. Fist it.

I comb my hair instead. I force myself to walk, one foot in front of the other. Body automated, I take myself to the chlorinated pool in the townhouse complex. The water is icy from the rains last night. I breathe in one-two-three and take the plunge. I dive, separate the water with the sword of my body. I swim and swim, length by length, stroke for stroke. Breathless, my chest is cracking, but I will myself on. The ambulance siren roars past my mother's house. It is softer than my heartbeat that screams through my chest.

Goosefleshed I leave the pool and head back to the house. I've killed just 40 minutes. The day lies stretching ahead. Time mocks me.

I survey my naked self in the full-length mirror. That Auschwitz look is disappearing, flesh is returning. The body wants to get better. It's amazing how, despite the abuse – the poisons, rat killer, pool cleaner, strychnine all cut into the crack and smack – I am alive and on the mend. My body is lapping up health as fast as it can, regenerating, regrowing – it anchors and grounds itself. Pity my mind lags behind.

I walk to the rickety typewriter. There is nothing to do but try to pin my thoughts, try to write and get it all down, try to find a reason, a meaning to all of this.

I roll that white page in, it looks at me. My fingers poised, my brain stills itself and then it comes, tap, tap:

26 November 1999
I am fighting to mute the killing thoughts. They will not go away, they bash, thrash over me. Like a group of unruly spectators, they pelt me with peels of reality.

My thoughts are my daggers, my head my enemy, I need to transmute this anger into something: art, love, anything – or it may kill me.

That's all I can manage today.

Landing up at my mother's home at the age of 33 shamed and disgraced me badly. I had lost hands down, six love: my husband, my sons, my home, my drugs, my dignity, my reasoning, my plot, my everything. Perhaps deep down it was the loss of my drugs, my most loyal and reliable relationship, that I missed the most. The severing of that relationship made me suffer deeply and caused me to feel incredibly sorry for myself. Once Joan of Arc, Yazmean Staggie, now a canary in a coalmine, my heart's trapped, stuttered – breathless, I cannot inhale, exhale.

It is as though I have truly fallen from grace.

On an empty day like today and all the ones behind me, I pick up the book *Disgrace* by JM Coetzee. I find it hard to hold onto words, concentrate (it's apparently a consequence of smoking crack). But I try to stay with it and read.

In the book there is a part where the lecturer who has had an affair with his young student tries to make an apology to the student's father. The father says: 'It's fine to say sorry, but what are you going to *do* about it?'

This passage penetrates me deeply. I know I have a bunch, a bottomless sack full of 'sorry's' to say – in fact, my whole life is all one big 'sorry'. Where am I going to begin and how am I going to change it? It all seems so gigantic, so unassailable right now.

It is the emptiness, the impotence that has afflicted me, that seems to be killing me; it is the post-drug depression that can only be likened to some dreadful ashy mental holocaust.

Trying to while away the days that drag on and on reminds me of someone who has been placed in a mental lock-up. I wait for anyone to tell me anything, for a sign, a touch, a bit of blood, anything. I mainly wait to hear from Boy 2 about when I can see my sons. He who was once my constant every-hour companion has now disappeared, etherised.

So in the end, to fill up my waiting, to stop myself from going completely insane, I write, anything – I just keep trying to write to keep a hold on something, prove in some way that I exist.

I do not believe anyone will ever read what I am writing. I am of the opinion that no-one will give a continental shit about this life of mine, this book I pretend to write. I mean, who will want to read about the sick, dark secrets of some scaly junkie who got lost in hell and then went to vegetate at her mother's house? Shoo wow! That sounds like first-class best-seller material.

On my travels through hell I had taken a folder with me filled with all the writing I had done over the past few years on my 'great' novel: *Don't Flirt With Heroin, It Will*

Marry You. (One smacked-out night Boy 2 had come up with that title.)

This was the work I was going to take to London, find a publisher, complete the book, sell it and make millions of pounds. Well, somewhere in between floor-hopping and hotel-swopping, I lost it all. On the morning that my siblings pulled me out of the 'Brow, I tried to run back into the hotel to look for it. Of course my sister, thinking it was another ploy to score more drugs, slapped me and locked me in the car. Leaving my work behind in that hotel felt much like when I lost my two sons … maybe worse. It was my *self* I left back there.

So it is to my absolute shock that one morning the phone rings in my mother's house and it's Dieter, the manager of the La Rosa Hotel.

'You're a very clever girl,' he says. 'I found this file of papers the other day – it was about to be thrown in the rubbish when I happened to look through it. I couldn't put it down, I took it home with me and read it the whole weekend. I found this number written on the back. I would like to get it back to you, but you can't come back here, into Hillbrow – it's too dangerous. Your mouth was too big when you were here and some people would like to see the last of you. I can drop it off for you – where are you staying?'

And so that's how I get my writing back.

Perhaps this was the first real sign of a miracle which hinted to my faithless soul that things might not be so bleak and heartless after all in the bigger scheme of things.

My truth and core were coming home, delivered in a truly unexpected and miraculous fashion. My writing was the only proof I had that I had died, but somehow, like Lady Lazarus, had survived death. The only record I had of the experiences I had inflicted on myself and endured.

The thought of my writing lost in some dumpster in Hillbrow seemed to make my life a meaningless parody. Useless.

Much like holocaust survivors who testified in Nuremberg and found some solace in their recording of what had happened to them in camps like Auschwitz and Dachau, the feeling of tightly holding my returned file of thoughts helped me believe that perhaps my catastrophic journey had been vindicated.

With that call from Dieter, it seemed a very tiny little pinprick of light had emerged. My writing was coming home to me! **I** was being returned to me!

I begin to attend NA meetings, every night. I am desperate for something. I spend my days waiting for 7 pm when someone will pick me up and take me there. Meetings are the only things I have to look forward to. Each night I come home and write down everything I have thought of. It seems to keep me alive, somehow.

'The addict is like a crab, pincer pleading, begging for more. The addict is a seething whirl of chaos attracting other needy little grubs to its furthermost deepest wants. The addict tries to pull everything in range down: it claws, grabs, twists, sucks,

always on the lookout for a chance, a scheme, and a way out.
Your neighbour may be one, the man at the petrol pump, the
suit in the office, the librarian at the book nook, the bespectacled
red-faced pharmacist who hands out your crisp white script.

'*The addict wants a soft landing, the instant solution; the*
magic bullet of everything is solved in a single microsecond. I
am an addict.

'*There is no real time in the addict's day; we are born of another*
clock. The addict pays no respect to the sowing and planting of
seeds. Seasons change, no worry. No waiting in patience for the
plant to grow, the wound to scab, the scars to fade.

It's all instant instant here – it's gratification that we seek,
no matter what.

'*The writer is a lot like the addict; life is the material on which*
we greed, feed. Guppies grabbing at scraps that spill, ribbons
of waste. Masticating, we gnaw on the bone of a tragic tale,
consume, digest and then regurgitate it on the white hungry
page. Now we have a story, isn't it neat? Complete. A whole life
reduced to a line or three.'

The meetings are where we congregate, they are housed
all over the city, mainly at churches or recreation halls.
Scott M Peck of *The Road Less Travelled* fame calls the 12-
step meetings like AA and NA the new churches of our
age. He believes they are the only true examples of real
community building, where people genuinely rally around
and work together to help each other stay clean, sober
and supported.

I don't think I would be alive today if it were not for those rooms and the addicts there who helped me.

'In the rooms of recovery we sit, white-knuckled, trying to recover. Our war stories are spectacular, like tales of heroes and knights on crusades to slay dragons – only thing is that the dragon we chase is heroin, yucky smack or crack, cocaine that makes us steal and lie and fraud and cheat and hurt ourselves and everyone else who happens to cross us on our hell-bent paths …'

Slogans rebound off the walls in the rooms: 'Just for today', 'Relapse no option', 'It works if you work it, so work it – you're worth it'.

Sometimes one can feel the string of tension in the meetings, where the desire to use is so strong that it sends some people out again, to do research and to fuck themselves up even more. The longing to use substances, it seems, does not disappear with time.

Addiction is not a straightforward disease like measles, where you have it, you cure it and it goes away, leaving you resistant, immune to future attacks. Rather, addiction is like an insidious cancer that stays hidden, it lurks waiting. Sometimes it slides into remission. There are people four, 11 or 20 years clean and sober who all say that unless they stay connected to the fellowship, they will use. Unless they stay vigilant and in the 'programme', they will use.

The meetings are like going for chemotherapy: they manage the disease, keep it in check. The space between using and being clean is just one little pick-up away.

There are days when I deeply long to use and I'm not sure how I make it through 24 hours. But I do, I stay on this straight clean road. Giddy with my own goodness, this is so unlike my usual self-destructive, self-sabotage pattern, I can scarce believe my actions and ideas. One thing I am certain of: the reality of using again and going back to the hell that I narrowly escaped from would catapult me into a hole so deep and black I can hardly contemplate it. I know for sure I would never be able to come back, there is not a chance of another recovery in me.

Like a newborn little worm, a skinless lamb, I peep and watch the world from my cave hole. Everyone seems so connected, so part of something: banking, driving, connecting, disconnecting, online, offline, dialling, sending, working, feasting, fucking. Oh little resentful me, I bury myself deeper in my womb tomb and thrash it all out on that ancient typewriter.

I collect clean time, one day at a time – 24 hours become days become weeks. I collect my time like people collect stamps or shells. I aim for key rings, tokens given at meetings for landmarks, 30 days, 60 days, 90 days, and as the days accumulate, so does my sense and awareness of self. Some call it consciousness.

One day I wake up and I listen to my 'voice' inside. It is not a voice that says anything very nice at all. It says: *'You're a failure'*, *'That's not good enough'*, *'Look at you – look at what a mess you've made of things!'* and *'See how dumb you are?'*

These are the messages I am feeding myself. I realise that if my mind is like a computer and all this info I am stuffing into it is manifesting itself, of course that is why I am feeling like a failure and a complete waste of time.

This single idea might be the greatest revelation I ever have in my recovery. Everything seems to fall into place once I make this connection. It is a real 'Aha!' moment for me. ***Whatever I put into my mind will manifest.***

I am nearly six months clean when I realise this and I make a decision to start reprogramming myself. I imagine a huge vacuum cleaner sucking everything in my brain away and leaving my mind an empty, blank page. It is a scary place to go, the place of nothingness. It is the bone skull place, the place of vultures and cannibals, the desert time, the night of the black heart. The place we go to when we are blind and dumb and all unknowing, when we wait for something to happen – a sign, anything to show us the way; that is the place where courage and blind faith are called to show up. It is the place where we leap from the edge of a cliff into the unknown, not sure if there's a safety net to drop into, or a wing to fly with – but somehow, by leaping, we find there always is.

I know this place well and I believe unless one goes there, it is impossible to experience rebirth. Christ says we must give up ourselves – and the Scriptures tell us: *'He who loses his life shall find it'*. Many mystics and gurus have said the same. I think this is really what rebirth is about.

CHAPTER 27

BABY STEPS

I have not seen my baby in six months – a whole half a year. A lot can happen in half a year in a baby's life. The last time I saw him was when he gurgled and stretched out his chubby little arms to me as I tried to grab him during the débâcle at the Klerksdorp cocktail party after the boys were taken from me. That was May; it's November now.

Today is a momentous occasion. Today I wear my red dress. Today I am to see my son. My heart is in my eyeballs when I enter Boy 2's new home, where he is playing happy families with his new life. From the corner of my eye I see a piece of the tea set that was given to us as a wedding present. I bite my lip and stop myself from smashing it. I must keep focus.

I have been shown photographs of Day and I now only recognise him from them, he has grown and changed entirely! He doesn't even notice me when I come in, let alone recognise me as his mother. No longer a baby, he's a toddler now, his large olive-brown eyes and chubby little cheeks, they are all like looking at a piece of foreign art for the first time. Oh my God, I have missed so much of this change!

My maternal feelings, once buried so deep in substance haze and rage, now rush to the surface. I want to grab him and hug and hold and never let him go. I hold onto the side of a chair and I tell myself: 'Calm down and just wait.' Instead, I know I shall have to let him take his baby steps and follow him with my own. He chases a piece of dust and waddles off. Step by step I shadow him, letting him lead me. My will no longer my own, I surrender control and let the moment happen. It is beautiful.

And then suddenly, from feeling invisible, from feeling useless and not 'there', I see him look at me. A grin envelops his little chipmunk face. It is as if the sun breaks through a dark and stormy sky. Everything, all my sweat, my struggle, the chopping of rocks on the farm, the meetings, the white knuckling, the sweating and aching of bones, they all come to a grinding climax. It has all been worth it for this perfect moment, when he looks at me and I am his.

It feels as if the fruits come to open on the tree of my new life. It feels as if at last there is a chance to start afresh. An hour later he lets me hold his chubby little body close to my heart. A week later he is following me around like a newborn lamb, bleating and calling me 'Mama'.

I start seeing my sons together, first for two hours once a week, which seems to be all I can manage. My system has been so damaged that I have to really be careful what I do now. But slowly it becomes easier and the time spent with the boys increases. I take another deep look into the mirror of my life. I can see that things can change, things are starting to move like a deep, dark river iced in sludge for thousands of years, that is now thawing. My life is starting to shudder awake.

All well and good, but much needs to be done! I am still sitting twiddling my thumbs at my mother's place, I am still largely non-functional. While I live at my mother's home, nothing is my own – not the sheets I sleep on, nor the cup I drink from. I know that I am going to have to change my situation in order to get a more workable space for me and my boys. I have to get a life. And having a life requires cash.

CHAPTER 28

GET A LIFE

Get a job!

I know I must work, this thought has been eating me for weeks, for months now. Everyone I see out there in the real world seems to have a function, a role and some meaning. I am meaningless because I am workless, incomeless and moneyless. If I need cigarettes I have to go begging from my mother, who gives me 12 bucks and then looks aggrieved, as if she's given me R1 000. She hates seeing me like this. I can feel she thinks: when is it ever going to end? Because I have come home, I am camping out at her place, day in and day out, I don't drive, I don't go anywhere, I don't work or speak to any people besides addicts at meetings who are mainly in the same kind of position as me.

One evening a woman who has taken pity on me, my sister's connection, invites me out to dinner at a restaurant in Melville. It's awkward because we don't know each other well, but I go along just to break the tedium and monotony in my life. As we walk through the doors of the restaurant, I see a sign on the inside of the glass window: *'WAITERS NEEDED. Apply inside.'*

Right through dinner the ad stares at me, goes over and around in my brain. Waiters needed. I think it's a sign for sure and it is specifically being addressed to me. I am so afraid to ask someone in case they say: 'Yes, we do need waiters – but we don't need *you*.' After all I have been through, my self-esteem is at an all-time low. At the same time, something else says: 'You can't serve tables! You have been to university, you have a degree, you're a genius – *you* can't do this lowly work!'

Finally at the end of the night, I bury my pride, breathe in deeply and ask for a job.

'You can start training tomorrow,' Nick, the little old Greek owner, snarls. (I later discover, after beginning to work there, that the 'WAITERS NEEDED' sign has been up for over a year, it never comes down because of the dreadful working conditions which make the turnover of staff so high!)

I am breathless, overwhelmed. I am so relieved that after all these months – in fact, years – of not working, I am finally going to be part of some labour force, receive recognition for my efforts AND get paid. I have finally got something to do other than sit and rot in suicidal contemplation at my mother's house, waiting for time to pass. She is visibly relieved when I tell her of my new plans.

The next day I walk through the swing doors of the fish eatery to begin training.

My first task is to peel squid. Their grey, slithery, mucous-like bodies slide between my fingers, I can't keep a grip on them. I pull the insides out, remove the cartilage and then wash the scunge, green defacatory matter, out in the purple-stained water.

I take the head, sever it from the body that squirts blue ink, take out the yellow eye and then put the tentacled squid head in another dish. I do this every day, for eight hours for a week.

It becomes the most meaningful thing I have done in years. I am somehow soothed by the squishy, glutinous squidge. I am in love with each clean piece of calamari. Proud of my work, I survey it like a mother might watch her child take its first steps. I have unfortunately missed my own baby's.

Somehow this task is meditational, healing, it is as though for a while my mind is hospitalised by the repetitive task. After a week I graduate to become a waitress. A big part of me would prefer to clean squid, behind closed doors. I am afraid of people, I can hardly write a word down, let alone greet someone and ask them what they want. But I know I have to walk through the swing doors from the kitchen into the restaurant and confront my fears. I really simply need to start generating some kind of income.

So I join the rank of servers, one who runs between those being served and those who prepare what is to be served, the kitchen staff. They are black and mostly illegals, Zimbabweans, Malawians, Zambians. The kitchen is the kennel of the abused. They are paid a pittance, work from 10 am until midnight. They get insulted with a measly 700 bucks a month, and all day they are on their feet, doing their dog grind work. Resentments flare from twisted mouths, grinding at oily tasks.

Outside in the soft surreal light against the sweet murmur of mood music, the eatery basks in its efficiencies. No diners who sit there in pretentious splendour would guess what goes on in the cockroach-invaded back. Chips spat on, vegetables chopped in weary hatred, cut and scabby fingers peeling scaly fish. Urination in the lemon butter sauce. It all looks so perfect out there under the dim, oh-so-subtle lighting.

I keep my history and my junkie identity under wraps. I am about six months clean and am terrified that anyone will find out who I really am and where I really come from. I know that the acceptance I enjoy would disappear in an instant if they were to discover that among them moves a sordid ex-heroin addict – that word brings terror to most people's hearts.

I am by far the oldest waitress working there: I'm 33, the others are in their early 20s and teens. It reminds me every time I listen to their carefree tales and laughter how time and youth have passed me by and how badly I have messed up.

I am working in the suburb of Melville; it is a lot like Yeoville was in the early and mid-'90s. It's an old haunt where I once knew a lot of people. They have all moved on with their lives, made money, bought houses, cars and have families who live in trendy picket fence dreamland. I have stayed stuck. In fact, I have regressed and I am terrified each day that I will meet someone I used to know and they will see that I am now a lowly waitress, they will see how lost and what a failure I am.

I watch the door of the restaurant like a hawk. One night a group of about eight successful movie industry people spill in for sushi. They are sunburned from a long day on set, laughing and raucous, they've wrapped up for the day and now they are hungry and want to eat. I know three of them.

I see them and run to the loo. I lock myself in. I can't go back out there. My sick pride just won't let me. I really can't bear them saying: 'Oh, it's *you* – what are you doing here? Working…? In *this* place…? Oh…' Awkward silence. 'So… um… what have you been up to?'

What do you say when someone asks you that?

'Well, actually, I have just stopped using heroin and crack for which I whored myself in Hillbrow, my children were taken away from me, my husband got clean and left me for another woman, she's blonde and very decent. I landed up on a homeless farm with robot people and now I am camping at my mother, who is an alcoholic and doesn't want me there, but otherwise, yes, well, I am fine, great, really …'

My fear paralyses me. Finally I realise I cannot stay hidden in the restroom any longer and I slither out. I avoid their table like the plague all night; luckily they are all pissed and snorting coke in the toilets and they don't even notice me. And that they don't even notice perhaps makes me even sadder than having them put me on the spot with awkward questions.

I have been working as a waitress for about three months when I decide I cannot stand the minefield in my mouth any longer. One of the worst consequences of using is the havoc it plays with the teeth.

My teeth have taken a real battering over the years: first the ravages of bulimia in my teens, then heroin, crack, malnutrition, two pregnancies in two years … It's like a jagged landmine at the back of my mouth. My tongue gets cut and bleeds along the edges every time I forget when I eat. I'm aware every day of the pain caused by my teeth and I am constantly reminded on a daily level of how far I have let myself go. The cleaner and more conscious I get, the more unbearable the state of my mouth becomes. I can't go on much longer like this. I will either get a hammer and bash out my entire mouth or I will make an appointment at the dentist.

As I sit in the chair, I warn him that he is going to be shocked by what he will find. He reassures me he has seen worse. The verdict is that three teeth must go, the rest can be repaired and he will fit a bridge for the extracted ones. The first bill is over R4 000, a fortune in my financially desert-like state, but I agree to pay him off with the money I am making from waiting tables.

Again, this is another example of a life-affirming action that I take. Although I am still experiencing suicidal thoughts, it really doesn't make sense to fix your teeth and then kill yourself. Fixing my teeth was like choosing to live again.

When I start recovery I have nothing – no money, no bank account, no house, no identity book, nothing that gives the impression that I exist or that I am alive.

Eight months down the line I have saved R7 000, which seems like a fortune. Each day after work I stash all my money in the pocket of my grey jacket from the homeless farm. I like to see the growing pile of money at the end of the day. Sometimes I fantasise and every pink R50 note represents a rock or bag of smack and I lay all the notes out on the bedspread and imagine going to the dealer and saying: 'I want R7 000 worth of the shit, 70 rocks and 70 bags of smack.'

Instead, I buy my own cigarettes, buy a new shirt, buy my sons pyjamas, drink coffee in coffee shops now and again … take the boys to the zoo, I get a bank account, I get an ID book, I buy a cellphone …

Something is happening, I can scarcely believe it! I am beginning to feel like a new me, I am beginning to *feel*. Not a 'shoo wow!', spaced out kind of feeling, but a small, almost imperceptible shift is happening. My spirit is beginning to feel cleansed, the toxins are starting to leave my body and my soul. The huge Everest-like mountains that once lay before me, impossible to even contemplate, are easing and becoming more undulating and beckoning, challenging rather than daunting.

There are little pegs in the tent of my mind, they are burrowing into possibilities of hope and fresh fertile soil; my foundation is being laid. For over eight months now I have not used a mood- or mind-altering drug or drink and I am beginning to feel the benefits.

My highway, which once comprised millions of byways and detours and wrong turnings, is straightening out into a narrow little village lane. My hands, that not long ago were scraping and begging and scratching, empty claws, my palms nailed to a thorny tinfoil cross – now they are reaching out. They are touching. I am working at my recovery like a pack-horse loaded by the baggage of my own creation. I am slowly, slowly shedding it, little by little. I am slowly, step by tiny step, starting to feel functional, slowly starting to become part of the real world again.

And just as everything seems to be happening and sorting itself out, as life will have it, I am thrown a curved ball of note.

CHAPTER 29

OUT AGAIN

'We are going to have to sell this place. She is never going to leave. We can move to the coast – anywhere – but it's the only way we are going to get rid of her.'

They are talking about me! By chance I happen to overhear a conversation between my mother and stepfather, who are sharing a drink and a gossip in the kitchen one evening. I freeze just outside the kitchen door and listen to their hushed conversation that slurs back and forth. Each word stabs me deep in my solar plexus. I go pale, my heart begins to beat overtime. I want to run in there, pick up a knife and unleash Yazmean to scream murder at them. Their words cut me deeply.

'You motherfuckers!' I leap in and stand before them. 'I heard every word you two just said!'

They are hardly startled out of their alcohol-laced daze. They stare at me and say nothing. Then my mother lets it out on me. All the years of pent-up anger and disappointment have finally exploded like a quart of milk stout. The words leap forth like a crazed typing machine, rat-a-tat – how I am the biggest failure and disappointment that has ever soiled this planet. How I have messed up my life and how I am busy messing up their home and relationship, that my presence is disturbing, how I am never going to amount to anything and how I am not welcome.

My stepfather stands beside her and supports her all the way. They tell me I am a manipulator, a liar and a thief and a total waste of space. I stand in the fluorescent light of the kitchen, I hold my breath ... my rage aches out the seams of my skin. I have been clean and trying to do the right thing. Now, just as things are getting better and my life is finally taking on some kind of meaning, this is thrown at me.

I try to bite my tongue, but the words rage out of my mouth, there is no stopping the diatribe. 'You fucking reptiles! You alcoholic fuck-ups! Where is your charity, love and forgiveness? Look at you drinking and fucked and in all your denial! And you have the audacity to say these things about *me!*' I reel in and out of rage, my tongue unleashed on the world ... 'I have changed, I am trying, I am working so hard to change!' I scream. They stare at me. 'Do you care?' I scream at my mother. 'Do you care, do you love me, have you ever loved me at all?'

My mother moves past me to the box of wine perched on the kitchen counter. She unsteadily fills her glass with her feeling-killer. I skulk back into my bedroom. I close the door.

That fight hurt me deeply and bitterly that night, but today I know that hearing those things was very important in catapulting me to the next stage of my recovery: packing my small heap of belongings, gaining dignity and making plans to move into my own space. If I had not been forced to move due to their insults, I may still have been stuck there, not taking responsibility and whiling my life away, living under my mother's roof.

'Get a hit, get anything to dull this pain. Get a hit!' The impulse to use on these painful feelings is so strong, I want to get trashed, get high, get away. I sit on my hands. I pray to a God who I'm not really sure of, but I ask for help. And I am not sure how I manage not to use, but I make it through the night.

———————

The next day, I go to work at the restaurant and I feel even worse: so low and down that my entire being screams to run out and use … I feel like I am dying, inside and out.

The restaurant is mausoleum-quiet. No customers, nothing to distract the thoughts that grow like sea monkeys. My head raves round and round with the same line: *use*. I have money in my back pocket, all I have to do is get up, walk out the door that leads onto the street, catch a mini-cab to the 'Brow and in half-an-hour I will be home free. The feeling, the desire to use grows more and more intense. It grips hold of me like an adamant Rottweiler. It will not let me go. The dirty cash burns into my pocket, the thought and smell and lure of Little Lagos grows.

I start imagining the route, the journey I will take. After catching my taxis downtown and then into the 'Brow, I will walk down the street, Soper Road, wave 'hi' to the hookers and then walk into the reception. I will get someone to take me to Room 306, the place where it all started. On the way up the Nigers will welcome me back like the prodigal daughter. I will go and visit Jon Bosco. Not Goodluck. I do not want Goodluck to see me back there, he will probably shout at me and chase me away ... Jon will sell me everything that my heart desires.

Like Bathsheba, back from her travels, cash will be the gift I carry ... like a millionairess, after I have announced my abstention from the stuff, I will order four rocks and two brown and I will get high!!! The thought is so strong as I set the tables, I find myself moving closer and closer, edging to the exit. One, two, three, I am about to just walk right out ... of ... here ...

But just as I reach the door, another voice takes over. Where the fuck does it come from?

'Consequences,' it says. 'Think of having to start this recovery deal all over again ... You will never manage. You will lose your clean time. The little respect you now have for yourself, it will all be gone in a hit, in an instant. You will lose your children, probably for good this time ... think of their faces, see their little hands ...'

'I don't care!' my mind screams back. 'I am tired. I am weary. I hate this. I hate being alive, like this. I am bored, I am sad, I am a loser, my mother hates me. I'm sick and I don't care.'

But the voice persists.

'You will never know what it's like to get better, to live the life you were born to lead. Your date with your children tomorrow *at the zoo – forget it now, you will never make it. If you give in now, it's all over. You do not see how far you have really come. There is so much that is going to happen in your life. Stay with it … you can't give up now.'*

'Oh, go away!' I hiss back. But the voice has me deflated. I look up. A customer walks in.

'It's your table,' says Helen of Troy, the manageress from her pale, pouty perch. I sigh. I pick up two menus. 'Hello. Can I get you something to drink?'

––––––––––––––––––

The customer I serve is Glynis, a woman I know from way back when. She has worked as a journalist and in 2000, is the features and deputy editor of the biggest-selling women's magazine in the country. She is friendly. She asks me how I am while ordering a plate of sushi.

Instead of doing the usual 'fine, fine very well', I land up telling her in minute detail of everything that's happened in my life in the last year. She is dumbstruck. As I finish off she looks at me and says: 'Why don't you write your story and send it to me? Maybe our magazine will buy it from you and publish it.'

To this day I have never quite worked out whether she was trying to get rid of this crazy waitress who had garbled her entire life story out while serving sashimi, or if she really meant it. Either way, that small statement changed the entire course of my life.

In fact, were it not for Glynis speaking to me that day, I would definitely not be writing this book right now. I have had the good fortune to meet a number of angels along my path, and Glynis was definitely one of them.

Today I believe there are constant signs and clues to what we should be doing, and people are often these signposts. It all depends on whether we open our hearts to these things.

I go home that night, place a pure white sheet of paper in the typewriter and I begin to bash, thrash my life out ... Five hours later *Six Weeks in Hell* is born.

Glynis loves the piece and her magazine buys and publishes it. A few months later, in September, just as I celebrate my one-year-clean birthday, the article appears on magazine shelves around the country.

Seeing my name in print and my words cover four pages was my proudest moment in years.

Now it feels like there is no turning back. Somehow, being published and knowing other people are reading my words ensures my sobriety. I won't be able to face the world if I relapse, my huge ego tells me!

Within a week of writing my story I pluck up the courage to visit an estate agent who rents out property and I pay my first month's rent and deposit on a one-bedroomed flat in Melville, Johannesburg. It is small and grungy, but to me it is the most perfect place I have ever seen.

My flat has a view. I am perched on top of the world, it seems – I look out over the hills of Westcliff and to the right, in the distance I see the top of the Hillbrow Tower. It sometimes winks at me at night but it feels like a beacon, a warning signal on a hill on the other side of my old world.

The flat is yellow-walled and dingy and I spend the week before I move in painting it white. When I notice the gas stove in the kitchen, a voice says: *'Ah, well, if this doesn't work out, you can always pull a Sylvia Path and gas yourself.'*

Somehow, knowing that I now have the time, space, opportunity and means, I never seriously think of killing myself again!

A few months later I receive a phone call from Glynis. *Six Weeks in Hell* has been chosen as one of four finalists in the prestigious Mondi journalism awards. The first piece I have ever written! I don't even know what these awards are, nor do I have anything to wear to the swanky hotel in Sandton where the ceremony takes place. And although I don't win, just being there and rubbing shoulders with the 'crème' of the industry gives me a feeling that maybe – just maybe – things will happen for me if I keep on with my journey.

CHAPTER 30

LIFE ON LIFE'S TERMS

'I am free. I am independent. I am taking care of myself. Thank you.'

Each day I repeat this mantra over and over again as I walk down the road along the Parkview golf course to work at a coffee shop in Tyrone Avenue. I have left the fishy, smelly Melville dive and now work mornings at a small establishment where coffee is roasted, sold and served.

I don't earn very much money, but the smell of coffee and huge amounts of caffeine on tap make me happy and hopeful. I have continued writing for the magazine on a freelance basis and I now begin sending my ideas to other publications. With each story I sell, my life gains momentum.

For the first time ever I am not setting ridiculous standards or unrealistic goals. 'Take it easy,' my better self tells me, and I listen. I walk like a toddler, little step by little step. Everything about me is small and I fight my ego and grandiosity at every turn.

———————

Boy 2 calls me to have a meeting with him. He has met up with a lawyer and he would like to discuss a divorce. I don't know why I am shocked by this news. Although he lives only seven minutes' drive from me and we see each other twice a week when he drops the boys off, he could be a million miles away. He is living a completely different life with Marie and her two sons and from the outside his existence looks content and perfect. I feel like the mongrel relegated to the dog kennel every time I see them together.

Suddenly the finality and reality of everything being over between us hits. I cry when he drives away from me and my soul aches for all the mistakes I have made and all the love I trashed in the name of using. But I know this is the way it must be, we are each other's worst triggers and our role as a couple has come to an end. He wants to move on and sort his life with this new woman and although I have no relationship replacement in my life, I must give our union up as graciously as possible. Plus he is providing a stable and loving home for our two little boys.

A week later we meet in the lawyer's office. It feels like I am moving in and out of a movie. I don't think I have ever quite realised I am married, and now getting divorced feels totally surreal and far too grown-up for me to imbibe.

The custody of our children is raised. I am prepared to bargain for joint custody. He suggests he takes full custody. In that moment I can see from the way he looks at me that he is doubtful of my sanity, of my capability as a mother. I become defensive. I cry and say I shall never give the boys to him. To be honest, my main concern is what people will think. It's the ego again. *'What kind of woman gives up the custody of her children?'* The voices scream at me, my mother's is the loudest of all. I am too upset to continue the meeting, the men shrug helpless shoulders and we reschedule.

Boy 2 catches the lift 13 floors down with me and on the way, he promises that we will share our children, that he will never stop me seeing them, that he will pay for their upkeep and he will tell no-one if I decide to give him custody. By the time we hit ground floor, I am beginning to see another point of view.

Two weeks later we meet again and I have had time to think. I am in no position financially or emotionally to take on the onerous task of two small boys on my own. Boy 2 is and has always been a father in a million: he was like this even while we were in active addiction. He is compassionate and caring and loves his two sons more than life itself. He also has a solid family who intervened to save our boys.

I love the boys desperately, but I know my connection has not always been that healthy and there have been times when I have really struggled with the motherhood deal. If I am really honest, I must admit there are days when I still do.

In a clear and rational light, it makes sense to give Boy 2 custody. We write up an agreement whereby I get unlimited access, I have joint guardianship and can share all important decision-making with regard to our boys' lives with him. We work out a plan where the boys will stay with me on Wednesdays and every weekend. But in the world we live in, a mother who gives away custody is still frowned on deeply by society – so although I sign the papers, I tell no-one. I am deeply ashamed that this decision is proof of my failures and inadequacies as a mother.

A year into the divorce, I realise just how beneficial this agreement is for me and my sons. It has allowed me to make a life *and* have the children – the best of both worlds for myself and, by all indications, for my two boys.

I don't believe all women are naturally great mothers. I often think maternal instinct is something I was given very little of when this character trait was handed out. Perhaps it is because I myself have not yet had a childhood.

Even today, with nearly six years' clean time under my belt, there are days when I struggle and squirm at the sheer burden of the task of dressing two little boys, feeding them, listening to them, answering questions (*'Mama, what is infinity x infinity?'*), playing, bathing, homework and then trying to finish up a freelance job, write a poem or an article in the middle of it all.

I guess this area in my life is by far the most challenging. Hectic deadlines on the magazine are a breeze compared with pinning down my six-year-old to get his shoelaces tied at 7.30 am, with the clock accusingly ticking 'late'.

Perhaps I am just too damn selfish and I have not been endowed with that self-sacrificing quality that seems to go hand in hand with mothering. Or perhaps more mothers struggle with these issues than would care to admit. But I do the best I can and thank God that they are healthy, beautiful children who are deeply loved by both their parents

I buy a car. It's the end of 2001. I have been saving money religiously from the work I do – writing articles and coffee serving. I have never driven, mainly due to that old man from *Repo Man* saying: 'The more you drive, the less intelligent you are.' I can't pick the vehicle up myself and so I have to have it driven to the parking lot in the back of the block of flats in Melville.

After two weeks of staring at it, I decide to venture forth and turn the ignition on. I turn it off and on again. A week later I inch forward and try to reverse. I stall it. I do this for a month on and off, forward and back. I look like I am insane! I have a real phobia about driving … I am 34 years old and every time I put my hands on the steering wheel, I feel completely wound up and ill-equipped. Terrified. It's like that moment before you get the courage to ride a real two-wheel bicycle when you are a kid.

Finally I decide I have to have driving lessons and employ a driving instructor called Leon, who barks and splutters instructions at me, like a deranged bull terrier – but he gets me going. I have to take a lot of lessons before I muster up the courage to book a driving test. A year later I get my licence, first time. Wow!

Driving becomes symbolic of me finally taking responsibility – for getting myself to and from places in my life. Today I don't know how I did without it for so long. People without transport of their own in this city can be really limited and lost. The car allows me to start really interacting with the boys – helping to pick them up, taking them to school, visiting people, finding more adventurous work for myself. It opens up the entire world for me ...

———————————

To celebrate my life and my progress and my third year clean, I found myself swimming with dolphins off the Mozambique coast of Ponte de Ourra. I managed to sell my story to a travel magazine – so not only did the holiday pay completely for itself, but I managed to make extra money for my efforts:

'Three pods of 40 dolphins, fins cutting through the mirror-smooth ocean, are heading in our direction. And all at once we see the most breathtaking sight: two babies have been brought along. They're really tiny, probably no more than a week old. I can scarcely contain myself as I wait for permission from the skipper to dive in. Quietly I slip into the tranquil water, snorkelled and masked. Beneath me I see a sight that completely blows my mind. A group of 20 dolphins is swimming a few feet under my unflippered feet. The babies – they ache right into my heart. A big grey dolphin slides slowly past, really close. She's ancient. For a second our eyes lock. Everything comes to a halt, I am truly and absolutely zapped, transported, primordialled ... entranced.'

Encountering those dolphins in Ponte de Ourra – so self-assured, free and unashamedly in love with themselves and life – really inspired me to embrace my own life with joy and new abandon.

By now, with life swimming forward, I knew I had to pluck up the courage to leave the coffee shop and somehow throw myself full-time into my real passion: writing.

I continued attending NA meetings – not as I'd done in my first year, on a daily basis, but once or twice a week – and while I found strength and guidance to maintain my own sobriety, I allowed the programme to use me to help other addicts, who – like me three years back – arrived lost and deranged from substance abuse.

I decide to work out the rest of 2002 at the coffee shop, and at the end of the year I resigned in order to follow my freelance career as a writer. I had spent almost two years serving cappuccinos and it was time to move on … The prospect of leaving my safety net was terrifying, but I knew I had to.

In December 2002, I meet Vee at an NA meeting. He's an American who's 15 years clean and sober. We instantly connect the day before his plane takes off back to the States and we strike up an e-mail relationship. In April 2003 he sends me cash to join him in London and I fly off on a transatlantic date. Because we are both in recovery, we decide to immediately get a blue NA meeting guide in London and cruise to two meetings a day, catching tubes, laughing and giggling like two clean little kids.

He's a really loud Yank, bling bling wanna-be Piff Daddy. He literally shakes the place and the pale English junkies wide awake with his booming: 'Brothers, sisters, family! My name is Vee and I'm an *addddi-i-iiicc-c-cctt-t-tt!*' I love watching faces as he roars: 'Family, by the grace of God,

I have not felt the nee-e-e-edddd to use a substance since 15 August 1987!'

I realise just how wide the NA circle is when I travel … you can walk in from nowhere, from the furthest corner of this planet, be an absolute stranger – and within an hour or two you feel completely connected, like you belong. The power of the fellowship and of recovery is incredible. There are more than 30 000 meetings weekly throughout the world today.

We spend six heady days together and when Vee leaves on the seventh, I have a day alone in London looking, watching, shopping and finally spending the afternoon at the Tate Modern.

Walking alone across the bridge spanning the Thames that evening, I realise it has been one of the happiest days of my life.

CHAPTER 31

MOVING ON

A friend takes me to a block of flats in Killarney and on a whim, because I have never done anything really grown-up before, I put in an offer on a beautiful renovated, Art Deco parquet-floored apartment. I am not serious at all and my offer is well below the selling price ... It's June 2003 and I have applied for a permanent job, also on a whim, at a magazine a few weeks earlier. The following Monday I get a call to say I have the job – and a few hours later I get a call to say the seller has accepted my offer. Oh my God, how insane is this!?

So within a week I buy property and get my first real job, where I have my own title, desk, medical aid scheme and retirement policies. I have grown up in a matter of days. I reel in and out of pure panic at the thought of the responsibilities ... How am I going to manage this huge shift!? But up to this point everything in my life has panned out exactly the way it's meant to be – why should these things be any different? So I draw on my faith in the universe and its wisdom and head off into a new horizon on a brand-new adventure.

In July I begin my job as a copy editor/journalist at the magazine and on 1 September 2003 the flat officially becomes mine, exactly on the date of my fourth-year-clean birthday.

In recovery they talk about the gifts and miracles of being clean and sober. Looking at my life as I open my front door and survey the 140 square metres of space I have purchased on the top floor of the building in this green-treed and peaceful suburb, and recalling the months on the homeless farm with zero to my name, I truly feel the wheel is spinning and spinning. My dreams are flowing in thick and fast!

———————

My mother does not look well on her 70th birthday. Her skin has a yellowish tinge. She is the life and soul of her party, though. The wine flows and everyone seems happy. I hang back. I have never been great at family functions. It's where I get to feel like I am adopted, a foundling who somehow doesn't fit into the circle. Alcohol, of course, does wonders at these occasions … Not able to indulge in the whisky or wine, I opt instead to glut on nicotine and smoke almost a full packet of cigarettes in two hours …

My mother stands up to make a speech. She really does not look well in this light. I must remind myself to tell her to change the colour of her base, the yellow-tingey thing is doing nothing for her. She turns to each one of her children, and says something appropriate. When she gets to me, the second-youngest, her eyes fill up with tears – as do mine. 'I am so, so proud of you, my darling child. You have come from such a place of darkness and you have done so well …'

In this moment, although I know these are just words, I feel as if all the approval I have been seeking from her in all the wrong ways throughout my life has finally been granted by these two simple statements.

I go outside for a cigarette, unable to contain my feelings, now mixed with pride and pain. Under a weeping willow I bump into my second-eldest sister, who sucks on a cancer stick. Tears stream down her face.

In my mother's party eulogies, she has barely spared a word on this sister. It has always been like this for her – my poor senior sibling, relagated to the Land of the Unacknowledged. I know she is weeping because the wand of invisibility smacks hard on her 'hoping you'll see me' heart.

There are many ghosts at this party: my father, my dead baby sister and here another one, my sister – alive, but in the family's eyes, dead nonetheless. Later, driving home, I realise that my mother can only acknowledge that which is spectacular. I have gone to insane lengths and inflicted untold pains to earn my spectacular place in this circle. The journey all but killed me.

Perhaps my sister was just never noisy enough ...

CHAPTER 32

CANCER!

My mother has cancer. Her yellow skin is not bad make-up. Her pancreas is infested with cancer. It's a cancer common in people who drink too much.

I can feel her terror. I try to comfort her ... I am terrified too. My mother, who once seemed to be invincible, is being eaten up alive!

Three days earlier I have given up smoking ... I have not imbibed nicotine for 72 hours. Hearing your mother has cancer is a good reason to start puffing again ... but strangely, perhaps because she has been diagnosed with the illness, I manage to keep my hands off the filthy packet of cigarettes that beckons and calls from each shop, each billboard that I pass.

My mother's cancer has spread like a lurky, murky unknown stain. The doctor suggests an operation. It is a complicated procedure – it's called a whipple. It will entail opening her up, cutting into the stomach and intestines and trying to remove as much of the malignant tumour on the pancreas as possible. My mother is not that old and up until now she has been in good health. The doctor believes the risks are minimal and my mother and the family decide it's worth a shot.

It all happens so quickly. One day she's my mother who is healthy, albeit drinking too much. The next day she is lying in an intensive care ward with tubes out of every part of her body. She is weak and cannot speak when she comes out of theatre. For the first time in my life, I realise that my mother may die.

My mother's stomach has been sliced open like an onion. She has been stapled together with 75 staples. She cannot go to the toilet on her own, she is in nappies and she hates every moment of it … Three days later she is moved out into a private ward and there we visit her whenever we can. I notice that after a week of being confined to her bed, my mother begins to strangely blossom. Her skin changes hue, it becomes rosier, her lucidity is phenomenal, she even begins to look translucent.

Although frail, she has a clean and beautiful air about her. Ten days later she is even more so, and then I realise it is the first time ever that I have seen my mother without a drink. There is no veil, no cover, no alcohol shroud taking her away from me. She is there like a beautiful newborn baby. When she looks at me she stares at me eye to eye. She touches me and I feel the connection. We are clean and new. Together, for the first time ever.

One afternoon I find myself alone with her, no other visitors. As the sun streams into the window, we hold hands and weep together. I tell her I am sorry for everything I have done to harm her. As I drive away from the hospital, I find myself feeling blinding love for my beautiful, sober and unslurry, unblurry mother. My mother, who was raised on hatred, and I, who was raised on flight. This time I don't feel like running.

Cancer is slow and sullen. It is secretive and hides and just when you think it's over, it rages back again, full force … My mother's cancer does not leave. It skulks. Although the doctors seem to feel it appropriate to look on the bright side, I can see my mother is being eaten up alive. The flesh begins to fall off her body and the pain aches from within, gnawing at her bones.

Although cancer is a cunning, ruthless death, there is a politeness attached to it … it gives you plenty of time to talk and mend and fix things up. I am given almost a full year with my mother, to come clean and make peace, while she slowly fades into death land.

CHAPTER 33

BELONGING

While I was using, deep in addiction, I moved further and further onto the outside, out of the loop of things. Not bathing, threadbare tracksuit on for two-week stints, skanky till it clung to my body like a second sweaty skin. Like a feral I lived in a cave, cursed coyote. Further and further, drifting from all that was once normal. I grew increasingly unsightly – orphaned by my own architecture. I sank. I drowned. I floated away. Bad land dreamland.

So in my recovery it was easy to assume that my great 'fitting-in' was imminent – I guess, like some prodigal wayward orphan, I longed to belong.

But as I stayed clean and sober and practised my principles, lived life and participated in an acceptable and decent lifestyle, I was to discover that standing outside the loop, and looking longingly through the glass at those inside, wining and dining at the table of 'life', was still to be my destiny ...

Previously my extreme, callous, psychopathic junkie behaviour alienated me from everyone and everything. Now my inability to fit in was also due to extremities, but this time the extremes of *not* using, *not* drinking, *not* smoking or partaking in a puff of a joint, at the very least. Abstinence and sobriety proved to be an alienator of note.

It was on one particular night that I felt my outside-ness, my different-ness more acutely than ever ...

_____

It was late September, well into my mother's cancer, when I sat one night at the end of the world ... 7th Street in Melville at a barfly's dive in the midst of the derelict, Jozi alternative terminally hip and fatally cool crowd.

There was Toxic, the local bleach blonde slut with broken fishnets and Clicks sale lipstick, skewed from a recent blow job on some or other metrosexual in the toilet of the corner eatery ... Next to her, her side-kick Toto whose penchant for paying for everybody's booze and Coke kept him well-oiled with friends ...

Me not drinking, me little Miss Teetotal, me fucking resentful, me so-o-oo so *so* bored sitting in a corner and saying 'No, thanks' to the alcohol oasis for the umpteenth time. 'Shee doeshn't drink,' slurred Toxic. 'She'shh the worldshhhh mosssht famish ex-junkie.' She collapsed in convulsive giggles.

I ached a smile, dredging it up like some defunct wind-up organ. It felt as close to the end of the world as I'd ever been. I closed my eyes, grinding my elbows into the piss- and semen-stained sofa. I clenched my teeth and – not wanting to sound whacko or, God forbid, religious – closed my eyes and whispered quietly to myself:

'God, I need a miracle. I need a miracle. Big time. Please send me someone. Someone to help me get through all this. Someone to distract me. Someone to help me with my mother's cancer, to

help me forget. Someone that I can get lost on. And God – please
… let him be really … sexy …'

I watched the window, looking onto the street like some bored tennis spectator. I watched that space and soon I forgot about my prayer.

Twenty minutes later he panned past. All six feet and more of him … Long, lanky, honey-brown dreadlocked man cruising casually past the window. Long striding gracious gazelle on some distant green savannah, he moved past, unaware of me and what his imminent role was to be in my larger-than-soap-opera life …

I watched. My skin reacted in little bumps. It was as if my body reached out of me, dissolved. My heart stopped dead. A squeal of brakes outside. A far-off ambulance moan. A gunshot … my heart stopped.

'Who is that?' I felt my breath suck in, I whispered to no-one in particular …

'Thatshhhh Dylan from Dublin … Liz's boyfriend.'

On cue, Liz appeared, mousey whining English rose on the frumpy side.

'God,' I gushed, not thinking. 'You have got *such* a beautiful boyfriend!'

Cold colonial stare – blank Tabula Rasa. Operation Nil Response. (I would at least have said 'thanks' or 'fuck you'.)

Liz was already drunk and invited the motley crew to join her at the bar down the drag. Needless to say, the invitation was not extended my way. Dejected outcast, I slunk home … Sulky skunk all alone. It seemed Mr Irish Dreads was attached and so I put all thoughts of the man out of sight, out of mind ...

The universe had other ideas.

———————

Sometimes in the eye of the storm, just when things look the bleakest and hopelessly hellish, a little cloud breaks golden and the storm delivers another, more promising shape ...

———————

I got up early the next morning. I wandered around the Rosebank Flea Market. It was a rare occasion when I had a Sunday free – my two boys with their dad.

'Hey.'

I turned around. It was Sam, another dreadlocker from London I had met at a party two weeks before.

'Hey, I got someone I want you to meet.'

I looked up. There he was. Mr Sexy. I felt my heart beat quicker, blood thundering through my veins.

I think I blushed and said: 'Ummm ... you are the most beautiful man I have ever seen.'

Or perhaps I just thought it. It's a blur when I try to recall. It was sure to have been something silly and achingly honest. But that moment in time really did stand still, like all good cliché romantic novels promise it will ... Time stood still, holding her breath.

We spent the next few hours walking around the market in the warm September sun and then the three of us sat down at an outside café. They drank beer and I drank coffee and I felt a connection to things again. For a while I could forget myself, my neurosis, my mother, the cancer and just engage with a new being who warmed up my space. At the end of the day he put his number in my phone.

It felt as if I had met a kindred spirit that Sunday ... for the first time in ages I had a spring to my step. Three weeks earlier, I had celebrated five years clean. Little did I know the months ahead would be the most challenging I had endured in my recovery.

When I told Dylan that my mother had cancer, he knew exactly what I meant because his mom, too, had passed away from the disease two years earlier. Looking back, it seems the dread dude had been specially delivered into my realm to help me through the dark time that snaked ahead.

My mother is really dying now, it's late November. I try to visit her each day. She can hardly walk. She has lost 20 kilograms over the last eight months. Clothes hang on her like she's a stick scarecrow, her bones protrude like some awkward Auschwitz corpse, about to be thrown on the pile. Once my mother watched helplessly as I emerged from Hillbrow – skeletal and hacking. Now it is my turn to watch my mother wasting away, and I am equally powerless. It aches.

I find myself speaking to Dylan almost daily about my mother. He tries with all his might to tell me that everything I am feeling and going through is OK. Some days I want to scream and force him to make me feel better … I hardly know this man, yet I feel myself latching on, heart skipping a beat when I see his number on my phone.

I don't know what is happening inside … I am falling apart, I am splitting at the seams. I want to use, I want to drink, I want to get high. I don't want my mother to die. I am scared. I am edged into a place I have never been to before and the strangeness of the terrain makes me feel like I am going insane.

'You are not using anything to displace your feelings, you are not even smoking,' he tells me. 'You are really doing well.' It feels like I'm in love, latched on, in hate and in fear of the dread man all at the same time.

———

On 30 November 2004, bile begins to drip out of my mother's static opened mouth. It is the pre-death black juice. She is in a coma now. Like a starving little fledgling, she lies eyes closed. My siblings and I gather round her. We hold a vigil through the night. My sister sings songs my mother loves, like *Danny Boy* and *Hi Lilly Hi Lo*. '*A song of love is a sad song …*' echoes down the empty hallway.

We weep together, our tears our unity, we are a family for the first time in years. Maybe the first time ever. We take turns wiping the black bile juice dripping out of the side of my mother's cracked and lifeless lips. Her mouth stays open. I imagine the bile is all the unresolved resentments, unexpressed dreams and unanswered prayers that my mother has held onto, so tightly inside her … she cannot stop it now, it needs to get out before she goes.

———————————

'I went into the bank yesterday, and asked the teller to help me clear a cheque – I gave her the whole "my mother's got cancer and I'm really stressed right now" deal. Then she said: "Oh, *my* mom died last year of cancer" – and suddenly I felt I had something in common with this stranger. She left and five minutes later the cheque was cleared. It also happened with someone I met at a magazine function three nights ago.'

'Ah, so you've finally got onto the Cancer Express,' Mr Dreads smiles as we sit on his couch, half-heartedly watching television. He explains that because so many people are being affected by the disease – it's almost like a global cancer network – there are millions in the same predicament. Like NA. Like the Junkie Express. The needy of the world sniff each other out, and extend their hands in help and recognition.

Dylan makes me feel like I am not alone in my pain. He does not say much, but when he does, his words are somehow reassuring and gentle and they make me feel less like a little black sheep bleating in the outback fields, about to be truly orphaned and all alone. Plus he's darned sexy and when I look at him, I can get really lost on his lean honey brown-ness … Just hanging with him helps me forget the ugly cancer right now in my real world.

On 1 December 2004 my mother takes her last breath. She dies. Ironically, it is only my ghost-like, invisible sister who is present as our mother passes from this life. I am five years and four months clean. I want to drink. I want to get high. Instead I cry. I can't phone Dylan, because I think he's with Liz.

———————————

'Don't you feel bad for the other woman?' asks Glynis. We're having lunch, it's a few weeks after the funeral and now, tired of talking about my mother, I have blurted out a few vague sordid details of my 'affair' with Mr Dreads.

'Bad? In what way?' I ask.

'You know that you're hurting his girlfriend … that you are helping to mess up her life?'

'I think that's *his* business, don't you?' I say defensively. 'I mean, *he's* involved with her – she's not *my* girlfriend. They are not married, they don't have a child,' I babble on. 'We are all free agents, she doesn't know about me and I am not trying to rub it in her face … I … It's really his business to sort out, don't you think?' The justifications go on and on …

Glynis looks down and picks at her salad. I know she thinks that what I am doing is wrong … how come I don't?

Later, as I sit alone at my desk, I'm disturbed by my apparent lack of conscience in this. Although it seems that Dylan and Liz have been grinding towards the end of their relationship for a long time, they are still a unit – at least in her eyes

– and I know that by societal norms, my behaviour with him is unacceptable.

'So just because I'm clean doesn't make me a saint …' I think to myself. Somehow it feels hollow. As much as I try to be uncaring about it, it begins to cause me deep unrest. Because I'm trying to live a clean life in all my affairs, the duplicity of this situation begins to eat me. I wake up earlier and earlier each morning – 5 am, 4 am, 3.30 am … I can't sleep. The restless mania in my cerebral cortex flares in mental tugs-of-war.

In reality, the triangle in my life is beginning to tear me apart. I like Dylan enough to try and accept that he is involved with someone else and the time I spend with him is the most enjoyable I have shared with someone in years. But I am an addict and, of course, I find myself wanting more. More. More. Maybe it's got less to do with being an addict – maybe any woman would start feeling this way.

I begin resenting that I am The Other. I find myself spending more and more mental energy thinking about the permanent fixture in his life: the girlfriend. I am constantly distracted … it's affecting my work, every area of my life … I am not the primary choice and it kills my leonine ego. On all-important occasions like Christmas, New Year and birthdays, he is her property, she has the first choice of him … I AM INVISIBLE!

It is such a familiar feeling, this standing on the outside, choking on alienation. It feels as if I have been doing it my whole life. It is killing me.

CHAPTER 34

PAVEMENT SPECIAL

The truth will set you free (you can't always get what you want).

I'm on my hands and knees, my face pressed into the pavement. The gravel is carving deep indents into my cheek. I'm trying to see under the solid metal outside a remote-controlled gate whether Dylan's car is parked in Liz's driveway. It's 5.30 am, and I have hardly slept a minute.

My brain has gone into a complete obsessive spin. He is with Liz. He's fucking her. He thinks I'm mad. Oh God, it feels like I'm in hell! I want to speak to him, wake him up. I can't. I'm locked out of the loop again. And now I have sunk to an all-time low of trying to put my head under a gate to see whether the love of my life is with another woman!

NO CAR!!! Thank God! I leap up. I look to see if there are any cars on the street. What if someone sees me leopard-shuffling on the pavement? This is so horribly embarrassing! I scramble back into my car, start the engine and slither off. I feel like Bridget Jones on psychoactive drugs ...

For a short moment I'm washed out with relief ... he's not with her ... I have found the truth and now I am free!

Then I catch sight of myself in my rear-view mirror. Is that me? Pale white around the mouth, dark eyes raving, pupils dilated, out of breath, it's the look I used to have after hitting a huge pipe of crack cocaine! And then my mind flips a cartwheel into new OCD obsession and delivers a new cancer bubble: what if they spent the night at *his* place ...? Oh, no, I can't go on like this!

I am finished. I am weeping. I am sleepless, deranged, a stupid wreck. God, what is happening to me? I'm nearly six years clean and I have never felt more unhealthy, more fucked-up. I may as well be using the biggest array of narcotics if this is the way I am going to behave and feel.

Obsession is like when all the space in the mind is squeezed into an uncooked spaghetti-thin hole and there is no end to the thoughts that keep going over and over the same thing, like a demented roller-coaster circuit. Obsession tangles and webs the mind into knots and detours and journeys of absolute *cul-de-sac* uselessness ...

And then a new thought slowly slides into my consciousness. This time it's clean and clear: *I admitted that I was powerless over my addiction, that my life had become unmanageable.* Step one in NA. I had so well understood this concept with regard to drugs when I first got clean, and now it is achingly clear that it must apply to this part of my life too.

Unmanageable? Oh, God, yes! I am completely and absolutely and entirely unmanageable.

I slam on my brakes and pull over ... Staring into the tomb-silent Sunday morning I make a realisation, the kind that should have orchestras of bells accompanying it ... *I truly am an addict* – it is by no means just the *drugs* I was addicted to ... it is *everything* I lay my hands on.

From the gym that I go to six times a week, to the coffee I gulp eight times a day ... to the way I work, speak, think, love and lose ... Mr Dreads has become a new addiction and here I am, helpless and powerless over everything I think, say and do with regard to him.

As addicts in recovery, we are often advised by rehab centres, counsellors and the 12-step programme not to get involved with anyone romantically for the first year in recovery. The thought behind it is that the feelings elicited from romantic/sexual relationships are strong enough to completely overwhelm the recoverer and take him or her straight back to using drugs again. How right they are!

Right now I feel completely raw, like a newborn baby, clueless about how to behave appropriately or control the flood of feelings and disturbances that are shaking every fibre of my being. Completely lost on love, like a smackhead drawn to my fix, I have been injecting myself on him and forgetting everything else about everything else, slithering and sliding on a dirty Melville pavement like a demented serpent in Eden.

I have made him into my Higher Power and now I need to do something to find my way back home, find my way back to me ... I see my eyes, my kidneys, my heart, my insides floating by, sailing down the street, away from me. I need to pull my being together, get real and try for perspective.

I decide I shall go to a meeting. I have been neglecting that part of my life badly. Filling myself up on a man, drinking and sucking it all up, forgetting about other addicts, my Higher Power, everything! No wonder I am acting like a maniac!

As things happen in my life these days, no sooner has the thought taken hold in my mind than I receive a call. It's Carey from the fellowship. He wants me to share my message of strength and hope at the same rehab I landed up in during 1996, when I was pregnant with Joy.

Over the years, there's one thing I've learnt: you never say 'no' when you are asked to share ... 'Yes,' I sigh, even though I really don't feel up to it – I'd far rather run away, hole up under my bed. 'What time ...?'

———————

'I was pregnant when I walked through these doors eight years ago ... it was winter and it was freezing. I was addicted to heroin and crack and anything else I could lay my hands on. Sometimes I wonder what would have happened if I had got the message back then and stayed clean. I think of how much less pain I would have put myself and everyone in my life through ...'

All eyes in the rehab are on me. They are sad eyes, bleary eyes, bloodshot eyes, dead eyes. They are the eyes I know that used to be my own eyes, the eyes of the zombie bone skull place. The group of 10 or so addicts glue onto each word I say. They listen to a fellow addict because somehow this 'junkieness' is the unsaid connection, the joiner that makes us all one real family, no need for explanations or negotiations.

I leave an hour later, grateful that I am no longer in the same hell in which these sorry people find themselves. It is good to be reminded right now of how far I have come … how good my life is today and how I never want to go back to the place of the pain of using.

On my way out a young, sad-looking girl, dark eye-ringed, who's been sitting apart from the rest of the group, approaches me … I can see she's really nervous. 'Uh … I was wondering whether … I mean, it's fine if you can't … if maybe … you could sponsor me …' she whisper-splutters it out and looks at the floor as she reaches out to me. It may be one of the hardest things she's ever done: ask for help.

And that's the other thing I've learnt over the years: you can only keep what you have by giving it away. And part of 'giving it away' is sponsoring (or mentoring) people who need help in their recovery. I have sponsored many people over the years; some of them have made it and some haven't. When I first began, it was incredibly difficult not to invest in the addicts' recovery and take it personally if they relapsed or failed in any way.

Over time and through trial and error, I have realised that I can offer my opinion and an open ear. But if the person decides on a certain day to turn left instead of right and go out and use – then I must separate, move forward and not feel in any way that their decision had anything to do with what I did or didn't do. It is not easy to achieve this type of neutrality and separation. However, I have found that when I do manage, a far healthier situation occurs. Counsellors call it 'setting boundaries'.

So I leave the place more grounded and with a new sponsee, Ann, in my life.

I decide to call Dylan. I feel as though I have been infused by a new-found clarity, strengthened in my resolve to choose healthier things for myself. The memory of leopard-crawling on the pavement earlier suddenly hits me again full force.

In my mind I rehearse what I will say, before I call. *'It's over. I cannot go on like this anymore. This is bad for me. It has made me mad. As much as I like you, as much as you have brought beautiful things into my life, I can't go on sharing you with someone else. It has made me crazy. I want more for myself. I want the whole deal – not little scraps and leftovers. Thank you for what you have done, but it's – it's over.'*

I dial his number ... 'Hello ... darling ... (oh God, I don't know if I can do this ...). *I have decided I can't do this anymore – it's made me mad. I'm not telling you to leave Liz, but I want out. It's over ...'* I feel like I have been swallowed by a sucking giant sloth.

Long silence.

'Hang on a minute,' he says. 'Something has happened. I can't really tell you much right now ... but please don't bale out now. Just be patient ... please.'

———————

Dylan and Liz are over. The information slowly seeps out from him over the next few weeks. I am terrified of the new space that lies before us. The terrain glares huge and threatening, it yawns jagged teeth at me ...

Anything can happen on this uncharted territory ... anything. There is no other person now to absorb the energy, to distract, to separate, it's just me and him. In all my plainness and vulnerability – in all my realness. Will he like what he sees? Will I?

I have to breathe really deeply and not let my terror sabotage everything we have. I have to inch forward, closing my eyes at times and just praying that I keep my big mouth shut and let my Higher Power do the work here ... And slowly, like a green, raw, unpetalled flower, I open and begin to bud. The sky does not fall on my head, like Chicken Licken.

CHAPTER 35

THE ACHY-ACHE OF ACHINESS

Sometimes I long for release from the relentlessness of reality. I may find myself thinking of a bottle of warm amber whisky – how it would feel if I let it slip down my throat and burn away all the achy ugly feelings within … how my insides will warm up, how my mind will stop whirring and how everything will slow down and be calm and lovely … Sometimes when I feel achy and crackly, this is what I long for.

On lonely nights, in times of soreness and disappointment, in weeping times, whenever my emotions are full on and seem to burst from my rib cage, get caught in my throat and well up in my eyes – when tears sting, when people I love die, when people I love leave me, when my children creep into my heart … when I'm angered, when I'm saddened, when I'm gladdened, when I love, when I hate … when I feel. Whenever I feel.

When I feel, I sometimes want to shut it all down, turn it, change it … click it off into something else. That's why I am an addict. Because I like to change the way I feel. That's why I haven't used, have managed to stay clean and present for six years now: because I am learning to sit with these feelings and, like a wave, let them ebb and flow in and out, up and down.

And once this happens, they slowly fade away. I am starting to know how to do this ... but I must never think I am too clever or that I have beaten this. As I become more clean, some days it is easy to drop my guard and believe I have recovered and that I can use again. It is a lie. For I know that to use now would be an illusion, a promise that holds nothing but dry twigs and whispered crackles on some far-off, never-reachable horizon.

Last night I lay on Dylan's bed writhing in neediness, not being able to say what I was feeling ... Longing for a big bottle of Jack Daniels to burn into my solar plexus and wash away my discomfort. He didn't know what to do with me, sitting on the edge of the bed, awkwardly touching my leg, my hand – me fearing he was longing to escape, but the polite nice Anglo-Saxon part of him making him stay.

He: 'Stay. You can't leave and drive into the night.'

Me: 'Please put the lights out. I want to lie in the dark and just cry. Alone.'

So he walks out the darkened room and retires to his book, somewhere away from my overwhelming emotion. I want to call to him 'Come back!', and cry and bury myself in every crease of his body. I never want to come up for air.

All the time my ugly voice is saying: *'You're pathetic! He's going to get sick of you!'* The voice tells me I have no right to feel, no right to be in this state and the more I fight it, the more the panic sets in and the feeling engulfs and all but snuffs me out …

I am so ashamed to show myself for what I really am. I am nailed to the bed, my tongue crucified – swollen strangled in silence. OH GOD, I HATE MYSELF LIKE THIS!

I'm out the bedroom in a flash, trying to grab my keys – escape, leave – run run run far away from this precipice of emotion. He sets me down like a child. He runs a bath for me, he cooks a meal. He does not back away and say: 'Go. You are too much.' He thinks I'm a little strange, for sure, but he walks through my pain with me, through my estrangedness.

CHAPTER 36

LEAVING

I watch him walk towards International Departures. His back is straight. His tallness sets him apart. I see his body get smaller until finally he's gone. I stand. I am empty. He's gone. I move. I turn around. I sense the cavern space. I know this feeling. Separation. I get into the car. Turn on the ignition. I don't cry. I don't feel like I'm even breathing. I reverse. I drive forward. I get into the right lane. I put on the radio. Michael Stipe sings how it's easier to leave than to be left behind. I cry. A little. I begin the journey home.

CHAPTER 37

MY BOYS

'Why is that man standing at the robot asking for money?' Day, my six-year-old asks, beautiful olive-brown eyes staring at me, trustingly.

I have just returned from the airport and picked up my sons for the weekend. We are waiting for the lights to change and a scraggly dirty man, obviously a junkie, approaches the static cars with a sad tale of some or other mishap in his life and why he needs money.

As he nears my window, I turn my head away.

'Why don't you give that man money?' asks Joy, my eight-year-old.

'Because he's a drug addict,' I say. 'He wants money to use drugs and I don't want to help him kill himself.'

'Why does he use drugs?' my son asks.

Oh, God! All the questions!

'Because he hates himself,' says my younger child. 'He's a shame man.'

———————

'Boys, I need to talk to you.'

I sit beside my sons on the carpet on the parquet wooden floor of my lounge as we eat a picnic lunch …

'You know I've been writing this book, and sometimes I have shouted at you because I have needed to have quiet time to think of words … well, I am sorry … I really am.'

They look at me, my two beautiful boys, open pages on which great stories will be written … their eyes aglow with love and life. My innocent little olives.

'I am also sorry for many things I have done – I am sorry for everything that I may have done to hurt you.'

I am lumped up. Any minute now I am going to spill over into a weeping heap. They silently get up and put their little arms around me, the younger one rubs my back …

'Do you know that the night that you were born … your brother rubbed my neck while you got ready to come out my tummy?' They love to hear stories about when they were babies …

'I love you, boys … you know that, don't you?'

They nod.

'I love you, Mama,' says Day, my little lion. 'I love you past space, past god, past *Star Wars*, past Cape Town. I love you 1 000 and 51.'

'I love you too, Mom,' says my beautiful Joy-Boy. 'But I love myself the best.'

Me too, boys, me too.

AFTERWORD

ENDINGS ... THE BEGINNING

'We shall not cease from exploration
and the end of our exploring
will be to arrive where we started
and know the place for the first time.'
- TS Eliot: Little Gidding *in* The Four Quartets

'How many words have you written?' he asks me every morning.

'Umm ... nearly 2 000, I've been up since 5 am,' I invariably say.

'Good girl.'

And he leaves me alone to write while he walks off and becomes a speck on the sand dunes that stretch forever into the blue sky horizon.

He leaves me to bash away at the laptop as I sit at a table, overlooking the awesome green-blue swirling, foaming ocean that laps at the edge of the mansion that I have been given to use while I write my book.

I have come to the sea to finish it and he is my silent companion, who wills me each day into meeting my allocated word count.

I think now how it all began, how all the miracles have taken me to this wondrous place – how I never thought I would be writing my life down, let alone a book.

When my mother died, after three long weeks of weeping and feeling like I was going insane, I said: 'Fuck everyone! Fuck the world! I am so sad and so alone now … I shall withdraw, write my book – fuck everyone!'

The following day I bought a sexy silver little laptop … three days later a publisher called and said: 'We'd like you to write a book.'

It felt like perfect symmetry, perfect meant-to-be-ness … and so it all began …

But writing the book has been an entirely different matter to the romantic idea of thinking about doing it. There are many days when I have sat and wondered what the hell I am doing this for, dredging up the sludge, the mud, the numbing gore of it all … Frozen at the keyboard as the unwieldy fist of a dealer punctures through the page and connects with my jawbone, my children ripped out of my heart, the withdrawal, the shaking, the lying, the stealing … everything that aches … why do it? Yet I do, every day, and within four months it is completed … It is miraculous how the words gather beside one another to portray a life … a whole life … my life …

As chapters gather, 'Should I be doing this?' still haunts me. 'What will people think of me? What will my sons say one day when they read it? Will they hate me? Is it gratuitous, egotistical? Should I be doing this?' I keep asking myself while my fingers tap-tap the keyboard as though propelled by something deeper.

And today I am watching that huge blue beautiful ocean, grappling with ways to end the book. Is that a dolphin I see laughing on that wave?

There are so many possibilities ... my children, Dylan, speaking to a fellow addict ... swimming in the sea , flying to the Congo ... laughing with my best friend over coffee ... sitting in silence and just breathing and smiling ... so many ways to end, I am overwhelmed with what to choose.

And then it hits me like a lightning flash: there is no *one* ending. There are just endless possibilities ... of life of life and life ...

And as I am right now, at the end, I know it's only the beginning.

THE END

How my strength is my weakness

Dylan sometimes used to say to me: 'You are so strong, you have managed to stop everything – even nicotine ...'

I would try to tell him: 'No. It is not my *strength* that allows me not to use. It is the knowledge of my *weakness*, the knowledge of my absolute inability to control my alcohol or drug intake that allows me to stay clean and sober. It is because I am weak that I find strength ...'

I don't think he gets it, very few people do ... It is not something that is easy to explain and most days I don't even bother trying to. I just smile inside and think: 'If only you knew just how weak you gotta be to be able to do this ...'

CREDITS

MELINDA FERGUSON loves her life today. She works as a writer in the print, television and film industries. She is happy to be mothering her two wonderful sons and wishes there were more hours in the day to travel, eat sushi and have more fun.